PhotoReading
Read this Book in 25 Minutes

This book is uniquely designed so that you can easily read it in whatever amount of time you can commit right now.

25 Minutes (Level 1) - Get the gist of this book in just 25 minutes. First, page through the entire book and read the table of contents, chapter titles, and subtitles. Page through the book the second time and scan for icons of Einstein riding a bicycle. Read the paragraph next to each bicycle icon. If you have more time, continue to Level 2.

30 Additional Minutes (Level 2) - Absorb the core concepts of this book well enough to discuss them in just thirty minutes more. Page through the book again. This time scan for icons of Einstein jogging. Read the paragraph next to each jogging icon.

45-90 Additional Minutes (Level 3) - Fully understand the PhotoReading skills by spending up to ninety more minutes. Page through the book scanning for icons of Einstein with a light bulb. Read the paragraph next to each icon. As you search for icons, remember what you have read before by reviewing titles and subtitles.

When icons are connected by lines, read all the paragraphs. Occasionally a note under an icon may say "Read Bullets"; this means you should read upcoming text that starts with a bullet (•).

Resist temptation to read all paragraphs next to all icons during the first time you scan through the book. Comprehension will be higher if you go through the book more than once.

You may desire to read this book word-for-word the first time. That is all right. You may choose different levels for subsequent readings to help you get more out of your investment.

What Authors Say About PhotoReading...

PhotoReading combines all the most efficient reading strategies—proven in university studies over many years—with what is now known about the phenomenal perceptive capabilities of the human brain.

It is undoubtedly the best accelerative reading improvement program available today. And, it is presented so that the average person can benefit immediately, and for a lifetime.

Dr. J. Michael Bennett, University of Minnesota
author of Efficient Reading for Managers

This is the best book for reading improvement ever written. Finally, one written by someone who truly understands the learning process.

Eric Jensen, author of The Learning Brain and Super Teaching

By following the PhotoReading Whole Mind System, you can enhance your learning and greatly reduce the time you spend regular reading. You can automatically single out the information you value and mentally highlight those passages you want to savor.

Charlotte Ward writing in Simply Live It UP

PhotoReading has helped many, including myself, to blast through materials at rates up to 25,000 words a minute.

Bryan Mattimore writing in Success Magazine

It's not just the fact that PhotoReading can transform your life in unexpected ways that excites me. It's also that Paul Scheele's book serves as a model for how to present new ideas well and forge new territory.

Peter Kline, author of The Everyday Genius

PhotoReading is a gem. It contains powerful tools for excelling in life. I thoroughly recommend it.

David McNally, author of Even Eagles Need a Push

PhotoReading appears to be a natural step forward in the evolution of human reading skills.

Win Wenger, Ph.D., writing in The Einstein Factor

PhotoReading is literally eye-opening... The goal: Let your unconscious take a snapshot, imbibing a whole page in a glimpse... It may well be the standard equipment for 21st Century SuperLearners.

Sheila Ostrander and Lynn Schroeder writing in SuperLearning 2000

If you read more slowly than you'd like consider taking a course to increase not only your reading speed but also how fast you absorb the information. The best resource I've found is the PhotoReading Course by Paul Scheele.

Jack Canfield, co-author of Chicken Soup for the Soul
and The Success Priniciples

We live in the age of the accountant,
not the poet...

...in the age of the politician, not the singer, in the age of the administrator, not the explorer. We thus live in an unbalanced world. Any development that redresses this imbalance is to be welcomed and applauded.

The PhotoReading Whole Mind System, initially developed by and now presented in written form by Paul R. Scheele, represents an excellent advance in redressing this imbalance. Paul's contribution has a number of noteworthy aspects to it. In particular, his work represents:

• A practical system for achieving an important class of accelerated learning skills.

• A significant refinement in the extremely important and ubiquitous activity of reading—in particular, Paul has decomposed reading into a continuum of choices. By so doing he has, in effect, identified and charted a continuum of cooperation between the two cerebral hemispheres. This places within the grasp of the well intentioned and disciplined practitioner a set of choices which are the natural (and largely unrecognized) heritage of every member of our species.

• The presentation of a highly learnable system which both delivers what it proposes and simultaneously opens a huge door to achieving a new balance between unconscious and conscious processes within the user.

Well done, Paul Scheele!

John Grinder
Co-Developer, Neuro-Linguistic Programming

I received the highest grade on every test!

I wanted to get my master's degree. I tried taking a course eighteen months ago. I was not able to complete it, because it took so much time and my grades were not good (C or D before I dropped the course).

I tried the PhotoReading method on some Navy correspondence courses, and it seemed to work well. I needed to test it for real, though. I enrolled in two courses at the local junior college in business law and marketing. I used only the PhotoReading whole mind system.

The results were astounding. With no more effort than just going to class, I received not just As, but I received the highest grade on every test in both classes. The best part was that I still had plenty of time with my family.

People at work and my family all say that what I am doing is impossible. I would have agreed with them one year ago, but instead I show them the transcripts to prove my progress. And still they do not believe.

I certainly am impressed.

Randy Now
North Highlands, California

I used PhotoReading to become a specialist in rheumatology and physiotherapy

I had thousands of pages to study for a critical exam. I PhotoRead and activated daily over a month, and I mind mapped the rheumatology textbook. When I took the written test, I both knew and felt the correct answers. My score was the second highest. I also did very well in the three-day, practical part of this medical exam, and I was the top student on the oral exam.

Ildiko Kiss, M.D., Zalaegerszeg, Hungary

What used to take me two hours, I can now do in ten minutes

As a tax consultant, I use PhotoReading to slash the time it takes to dig information from the 33-volume IRS code. I find the section I want in the index. Then I PhotoRead that section—30-40 pages. Immediately the answers appear to jump off the page.

Fred Fredricks, Hong Kong

I'm more productive at work

I PhotoRead my software manuals. Now, when I program, the code seems to come out of my head, and I hardly ever stop to look in the manuals as before. I intuitively know the program will work, and it does. Previously I would have written a bit, tested it, tweaked it, referred to the manual...

Lou Wilson, Middlesex, England

I got a 100% salary increase

After learning PhotoReading, I lowered my reading backlog by 40 books in the next 28 days. I applied the PhotoReading techniques to a business presentation and got a job offer with a 100% salary increase.

Joan Jiménez, General Council of Education, Rio Piedras, Puerto Rico

My business doubled

As a business owner, I am always looking for ways to increase my sales. I PhotoRead marketing books that I hadn't found time to read, and then put together a new sales piece that yielded twice what I had done before.

John DuCane, St. Paul, Minnesota

I wrote 20 pages of notes without opening the book again

Yesterday I PhotoRead a law book. This morning I activated it. I then decided to make just a few notes... I am astounded!

Ray Simons, Las Vegas, Nevada

PhotoReading

by Paul R. Scheele

 Learning Strategies Corporation

Innovating ways for you to experience your potential

2000 Plymouth Road
Minnetonka, Minnesota 55305-2335 USA

Toll-Free 1-888-800-2688 • 1-952-767-9800
Fax 1-952-475-2373

Mail@LearningStrategies.com
www.LearningStrategies.com

Learning Strategies Corporation
2000 Plymouth Road
Minnetonka, Minnesota 55305-2335 USA
Toll-Free: 1-888-800-2688 ~ 1-952-767-9800 ~ Fax: 1-952-475-2373
Mail@LearningStrategies.com
www.LearningStrategies.com

Learning Strategies Corporation is a Private Vocational School licensed
by the Higher Education Services Office of the Minnesota Department of Education.

Library of Congress Control Number: 2007924535

ISBN-13: 978-0-925480-68-2

Fourth Edition
Copyright 2007 by Learning Strategies Corporation
(First Edition: Copyright 1993)

PhotoReading®

Table of Contents

How to Read this Book • Foreword

Acknowledgments • About the Author

Part One: Increase Your Choices

Part Two: Learn the PhotoReading Whole Mind System

Part Three: Develop and Integrate Your Skills

Foreword

Welcome to the most innovative reading program available. PhotoReading goes beyond mere speed reading. It is an educational experience that taps your mind's vast resources. It explores and expands your own potential.

We live in an age when too little time and too much information compete. If we are to succeed, we require new skills for processing and learning from information. PhotoReading is about working with the greatest information processing device known to mankind: the human mind.

In this book you will learn techniques for using the powers of your whole mind. PhotoReading will teach you how to not just read faster but *learn* at speeds many times faster than before.

When you learn PhotoReading, you will experience what might sound impossible. You will PhotoRead the written page at rates exceeding a page per second, directing information into the expanded processing capabilities of your brain. There the information connects to your prior knowledge and becomes useful in accomplishing your purposes. You get your reading done in the time you have available, at a level of comprehension you need.

With the PhotoReading whole mind system, you will develop extraordinary communication with the your brain. PhotoReading bypasses the limited capabilities of the conscious mind and helps you find your personal genius.

This book contains the revised five-step PhotoReading whole mind system now being taught worldwide in the PhotoReading seminar and the PhotoReading Retreat. The steps of Prepare, Preview, PhotoRead, Activate, and Rapid Read have been reorganized into Prepare, Preview, PhotoRead, Postview, and Activate with the step of Rapid Read woven into Activate.

We have seen that this change has helped:

• improve access to the processing power of your whole mind for greater comprehension and recall,

• decrease interference from the limitations of the conscious mind for greater speed and confidence, and

• ease application across all types of written materials, especially electronic text, helping you gain mastery over anything you have to read.

Acknowledgments

As this Fourth Edition of *PhotoReading* goes to press, PhotoReading continues to evolve thanks to the continuing work of over a hundred dedicated people. I especially acknowledge Master PhotoReading Instructor Lynette Ayres who worked with me to reorganize the PhotoReading whole mind system.

I acknowledge the spirit and commitment of the certified PhotoReading instructors. They are today's pioneers, forging a new form of education. They significantly influence PhotoReading by creatively exploring new ways to teach and use PhotoReading.

The most important contributor to PhotoReading is the PhotoReading student, whose insights and breakthroughs are invaluable to PhotoReading's continued evolution.

Kudos to the people of Learning Strategies Corporation and our worldwide marketing associates for their diligent work in helping spread the word about PhotoReading. Thanks to them, we have hundreds of thousands of additional PhotoReaders around the world.

I salute all those who contributed to the early development of PhotoReading. The names of these talented and insightful associates are on permanent record in previous editions of this book.

Finally, I acknowledge you, the reader, for recognizing you have the power within to accomplish most anything you desire. You make breakthroughs such as PhotoReading a reality. Please write me of your successes.

Paul R. Scheele

About the Author

Paul R. Scheele works to transform the lives of people around the globe. In more than thirty years his work has touched over one million people. His dynamic programs cultivate human potential and awaken the genius mind in everyone. He teaches how to increase health and wealth, improve relationships, and implement new knowledge with ease. Quite profoundly, he inspires individuals and organizations to go beyond conventional thinking into what is truly possible.

Paul educates audiences to access their full potential using powerful learning strategies. His unique combination of expertise includes a Bachelor of Science in Biology from the University of Minnesota, a Masters Degree in Learning and Human Development from the University of St. Thomas, doctoral studies in Leadership and Change from Antioch University, and a rich background in neuro-linguistic programming (NLP), accelerated learning, and preconscious processing.

Paul is co-founder of Learning Strategies Corporation, a premier developer of self-improvement, education, and health training programs. Paul has designed and delivered over fifty different programs relating to professional and personal development. He is the author of another book, *Natural Brilliance*. His work has been translated into eighteen languages.

Paul fosters the achievement of desired outcomes and the realization of greater abundance in people's lives. Learning "how to learn" from him enhances everything you study, including other training programs. His teachings are scientifically-based and access the highest realms of human potential. Paul's programs contribute the critical knowledge that makes all the difference in attaining real success in today's ever changing and challenging world.

He is an insightful public speaker and consultant to companies and organizations worldwide.

Paul lives with his wife Libby in a suburb of Minneapolis, Minnesota. They have three sons, Ben, John, and Scott.

He may be reached by writing Learning Strategies Corporation, 2000 Plymouth Road, Minnetonka, Minnesota 55305-2335 or email at Mail@LearningStrategies.com.

Paul lovingly dedicates his work to his family.
Their passion for reading and zest for life inspires and
motivates him every day.

Part One:

Increase Your Choices

1

The Origins of PhotoReading

PhotoReading at 25,000 words a minute means you could "mentally photograph" this book in fewer than three minutes. Although this may sound like a radical new idea, the concept existed at least a hundred years before I coined the term *PhotoReading*. You can find evidence that such mental processing is possible and has been used in diverse settings from military training and martial arts to ancient religious traditions.

The challenge is not in deciding whether PhotoReading is possible. The challenge is how to teach you, as an individual reading this book, to effectively transfer this natural ability into daily applications for reports, journals, newspapers, books, web pages, or whatever you want to read.

My background in neuro-linguistic programming and accelerative learning gave me a way to meet that challenge. The PhotoReading whole mind system has been learned by others around the world, and now the time is right for you to learn it, too. The story that follows explains how it all started.

Seven years after graduating with a science degree from the University of Minnesota, I took a speed reading test. I scored 170 words a minute at 70 percent comprehension. I was embarrassed when I realized my 16-plus years in public schools left me below average in reading skills and an expert at putting off reading.

I thought that to read properly I must start on the first word of a text and slog through to the end. I must concentrate on seeing all the words correctly, make sense of them as I went along, and remember what they said. I also believed the ultimate measure of my reading effectiveness was total recall and critical analysis of meaning.

I did not question my definition of reading. I felt stuck at slow speeds. I knew that the faster I read, the worse my comprehension became.

After seven years of professional life as a human resource development consultant, I had made no improvement in my reading skills.

In 1984, the logical solution meant enrolling in a speed reading course. After five weeks of training, my speed reading scores averaged 5,000 words a minute at 70 percent comprehension.

During one of the class sessions, a young woman sitting next to me lamented being stuck at 1,300 words a minute through ten weeks of classes. I suggested to her, "Imagine what it would be like if you could break through to higher speeds now." On her next book, her speed reading reached over 6,000 words a minute with higher comprehension test scores than ever before.

As great as that sounds, speed reading did not appeal to me. Pushing my eyeballs down the page soon became unrewarding drudgery. Three months after leaving the course, I rarely used the techniques but remained intrigued about the mind's potential for processing written words.

I began realizing my problem—I felt trapped between two opposing belief systems. One belief came from the elementary education model of reading. An opposing belief came from knowing that the human mind can achieve far more magnificent results. The same trapped and confusing feeling grabbed me once during private pilot's training.

I remember when my instructor took me up to eight thousand feet and told me to fly at a minimum airspeed just as I would when landing. To do so, I slowed down the engine and pulled back on the control yoke to maintain my altitude.

Soon, the nose of my plane pointed almost straight up. The wind flowing over my wings no longer created enough lift to hold up the airplane. It could not fly so it dropped out of the sky like a rock, diving straight down toward the ground.

Terrified, I immediately began pulling back on the control yoke, trying desperately to get the nose up and fly the plane. This made things much worse. My instructor seemed to enjoy watching my panic.

Why wasn't it working? Why wouldn't the plane fly? Diving toward the ground at an accelerating rate, my instructor calmly said, "Push forward."

I knew he did not have a clue about our problem. While I tried to lift the plane up by the control yoke, he was telling me to dive deeper into the ground? Clearly he had lost his mind.

The plane entered a tail spin, and the earth became a spinning blur rushing toward us. Every part of me resisted his command as he insisted more firmly, "Push into the spin!"

Finally, my instructor broke my white-knuckled grip and pushed the control yoke forward. This push immediately smoothed out the wings and elevator section of the tail, which corrected the airflow over them and generated lift. The plane stabilized and slowly he pulled back the control yoke to regain altitude, leaving my heart in my throat. Wow.

What connection does this have to reading? Throughout my life I read only as fast as I could comprehend the words on the page. Every time I went too fast to comprehend, I grabbed control and pulled back as a fear reaction. I was afraid I would fail as a reader if I did not understand everything. My attempted strategies to read better and faster only made things worse. I was caught in the spin, and reading felt like nose-diving my airplane into the ground.

Have you ever wished for a mentor to come along and pull you out of a nosedive? I did. Unfortunately, I did not realize a larger, more powerful capacity of mind could solve my reading problem. Fortunately, miracles happen. Several events in the next few years shaped a new direction for me.

In the fall of 1984, I entered graduate school to study adult learning and human development technologies. I wanted to know how people learn most effectively. My company, Learning Strategies Corporation, was over three years old with many clients who could benefit from my studies. I was also strongly motivated to improve my own skills as a learner.

While attending different seminars and courses, I heard about an instructor from a speed reading school in Phoenix, Arizona. The instructor had suggested a bizarre experiment to one of his classes. After flipping pages upside down and backwards to learn eye-fixation patterns, he instructed the students to take a comprehension test on the book, just for the fun of it. Their scores turned out to be the highest the class had ever achieved. Was it a fluke? The instructors at the school hypothesized that maybe they were turning the page into a stimulus that is processed subliminally.

About the same time I heard that hypothesis, I attended a workshop with Peter Kline, an expert in accelerative learning. When I told him about my interest in researching breakthroughs in reading, he offered me a challenge. A client of his, IDS/American Express, wanted a speed reading application of accelerative learning. Suddenly, a consulting job, my master's degree work, and my passion for learning landed in one nice package on my lap.

In the fall of 1985, I began background research into studies of subliminal perception and preconscious processing. Significant research evidence suggested humans possess a preconscious processor of the mind that can absorb visual information without involving the conscious mind. I experimented with using the eyes and the preconscious processor in special ways on written materials. I dubbed this concept of "mentally photographing" the printed page *PhotoReading*.

I devoted my full time to designing a seminar based upon the accelerative learning model, expert strategies of rapid reading, the human development technology of neuro-linguistic programming, and studies on preconscious processing. Soon the PhotoReading seminar was born.

One of my experiments involved returning to the speed reading school I had attended. I asked the teacher for several books and tests. After PhotoReading one of the books at 68,000 words a minute, I demonstrated 74 percent comprehension on the same type of written test I had used a few years earlier.

Too good to be true? Compared to reading or speed reading, it was too good to be true. PhotoReading, however, was neither. Something powerful was happening, and the school confirmed the results.

In January and February of 1986, I taught the first six experimental seminars—one to IDS and five to clients of my company. Participants stood up during class to describe many immediate payoffs including reduced stress, startling improvements in memory, fluid reading skills, top grades on school tests, increased wins for salespeople and trial attorneys, and more.

Inspired by the participants' excitement, I worked on refining the curriculum design and teaching materials with my business associates. On

May 16, 1986, the Minnesota Department of Education licensed Learning Strategies Corporation as a private vocational school after reviewing the PhotoReading seminar curriculum and our business practices.

When the President of the United States of America declared the 1990s the "decade of the brain," he invited an explosion of new research in cognitive science. The resulting breakthroughs in our understanding of how the brain processes information have offered unprecedented support for the pursuit of new approaches to learning. PhotoReading has earned international recognition for its innovations to education.

Instructors specially trained and certified by Learning Strategies Corporation, continually upgrade PhotoReading into a life-transforming human development experience that incorporates the latest in brain research to help achieve success. It is offered worldwide through live seminars and a self-study course, and is supported with telephone and online coaching.

PhotoReading helps you acquire new skills to increase reading efficiency. As most PhotoReaders admit, however, PhotoReading transforms more than reading skills. The PhotoReading whole mind system directs you to "push into the spin" and discover the natural genius residing within you. This means you fly smoothly through information instead of spinning out of control. This book will help deliver the system to you in clear, step-by-step instructions.

A preview of what is to come

The five steps to the PhotoReading whole mind system have evolved to Prepare, Preview, PhotoRead, Postview, and Activate.

The system appears as a set of steps in sequence, although it is actually a set of options that can be used in any order appropriate to your needs. It models the strategies used by highly skilled readers.

The secret power in the system is not in the techniques, but in the shift in perspective the techniques engender. To use the system and achieve your goals, you must confront the compulsion to habitually apply inefficient strategies.

In the pages that follow, you will examine the limitations that bind you to your present capacities. You will gain ways to bypass the limited processing capabilities of the conscious mind and connect with the expanded processing capabilities of your brain in which your natural genius resides. The simple behaviors you learn can be used right away.

Right now, you can only imagine the good that can take place as you use more of your innate talents. Over the years of teaching Photo-Reading to thousands worldwide, I have witnessed many personal and professional transformations. Here are a few examples:

• A high school student PhotoRead the dictionary repeatedly and dramatically improved her vocabulary score on SAT exams.

• An attorney uses PhotoReading to quickly locate vital facts in huge law books. Now, instead of spending half-an-hour in a typical visit to the law library, he spends five minutes.

• A technical writer PhotoRead a client's software systems manual before his initial meeting with the project engineers. He was able to talk knowledgeably about the system with only fifteen minutes of preparation time.

• A computer service technician consistently locates key information in reference manuals within seconds.

• An attorney took three minutes to PhotoRead a three hundred-page legal manual from the Department of Transportation. He instantly turned to the one paragraph in the text that included the information he needed to win a case. The state's expert witness, who had been unable to find this paragraph, was stunned as he saw the attorney perform this feat.

• A waste water specialist for E.I. Dupont had to read a three-inch stack of federal regulations from the Occupational Safety and Health Administration (OSHA) in preparation for a meeting. During a 35-minute flight to the meeting, he PhotoRead the documents. During the meeting, he correctly stated that OSHA would no longer accept water treatment data that was more than three years old—a technical point buried in the regulations he had just PhotoRead.

• A business consultant visited the city library to PhotoRead industry trade journals before his initial meeting with a prospective corporate client. Her knowledge on industry trends, key problems, and innovative practices gave her the edge over other consultants being interviewed. She won the contract.

• A college student used PhotoReading to successfully complete his degree, gain employment at a high-tech firm, and then rise in the ranks of new hires. He claimed he owed his success to the advantages PhotoReading gave him.

• A group of high school students from Puerto Rico used PhotoReading to win medals in an international Mental Olympics contest.

• In his acceptance speech for top honors, a short story writer announced that PhotoReading was the secret ingredient for his excellence in creativity and writing style.

These examples only begin to express the benefits. Our clients also say that PhotoReading helps them to write reports, pass critical exams, excel in school courses, finish degrees, sail through meetings, earn promotions, and do more of the reading they really want to do for enjoyment.

The only requirements for PhotoReading are a willingness to experiment, use new ideas, relax, and play. Then the full genius within you will be released. Become like a child—naturally curious, wondering, experiencing, discovering—and a whole new world of easy reading will unfold.

Reading will become a new source of personal and professional power. You will explore written materials with new levels of effectiveness. The benefits offered by the PhotoReading whole mind system will help you create a quality of life that will delight and surprise you.

The next chapter gets you set and ready to go.

A student improved his high school math grade from a D to a B in one semester. He said that PhotoReading math books must have given him ways to do problems better. Another student PhotoRead a variety of books before preparing a theme paper. The teacher wrote on her paper, "A+ Your writing style improved overnight. What did you do?!"

Several musicians have reported uses of PhotoReading music. They find that PhotoReading musical scores a day before first playing the music makes the first run through much easier—as if they have already practiced the piece.

A doctor of psychology from Mexico was asked to present her twenty-page research paper to a conference in California. Because it was written in Spanish, she would have to translate the paper as she spoke. Although she was bilingual, she had always found it difficult to speak English from Spanish writing. She PhotoRead the Spanish-English dictionary several times the day and night before her presentation. During her speech, she spoke fluently without any confusion whatsoever. She reported being relaxed and completely comfortable the entire time.

A gardener found it easier to recognize plants after PhotoReading a guide.

A high school English teacher used the PhotoReading whole mind system to prepare for an American literature unit on Hemingway. She PhotoRead all the commentaries on Hemingway's writing, plus all books he wrote including the two the class unit would cover. In addition, she rapid read the two books. She surprised herself as the material activated spontaneously during her lectures. Her knowledge of the subject contained rich examples, giving the class depth that surpassed any unit she had ever taught.

A mountain biker flies down hills faster, because his field of vision opened up. "I trust my inner knowing. I feel relaxed, and the bike floats over bumps."

A new employee attended a meeting on the first day of her job. She had spent a few minutes PhotoReading reports before the meeting and contributed to the conversation as if she had been working there forever. "The meeting was an activation of the materials. I don't know who was more surprised, me or my new coworkers!"

Two friends read novels in front of the fireplace during the evenings while on a skiing vacation. The PhotoReader brought five novels; the other just one.

A chemist discovered that PhotoReading his college textbooks helped develop his understanding of charts which in the past presented problems.

Two friends played tennis for years. One of them took the PhotoReading course and PhotoRead five books on tennis. His game immediately improved so significantly that the other man was stunned. When he discovered how the miraculous improvement occurred, he signed up for the next PhotoReading class. The end result was the same improvement in his own tennis game.

A beginning PhotoReader PhotoRead ten books a day for several weeks so that the process became second nature. One morning he PhotoRead a book on how quantum physics relates to the brain. That afternoon, during a slow period of a Minnesota Vikings football game, he spontaneously imagined thoughts, ideas, concepts, principles, and theories about physics. Several days later, he told colleagues of his experience, one of whom was a physics expert. After quizzing the PhotoReader, the physics expert said that the PhotoReader, as a lay person, knew a heck of a lot about physics. The PhotoReader had tremendous confidence that, if he went back to the book and activated it, he would easily gain additional knowledge since PhotoReading had given him a solid basis of understanding.

A successful real estate developer was a true self-made man. He dropped out of school in the tenth grade and never looked back. In his entire life of fifty years, he had read a mere three books. After learning PhotoReading, he reported, "It's just wonderful. I've read a dozen books in the last two weeks, and I'm loving it. The PhotoReading course has been one of the most enjoyable experiences of my life." For many years, he never considered himself a person who could learn. Through PhotoReading, he demonstrated he could.

2

Old Reading Habits or New Reading Choices

Take a moment to paint a vivid mental picture of the kind of reading materials you encounter regularly. Among the possibilities are:

- Websites, blogs, RSS feeds, and other electronic files
- Magazines or trade journals
- Newspapers
- Mail and email
- Memos
- Owner's manuals or reference guides
- Training materials
- Reports
- Proposals or sales literature
- Specification sheets
- Nonfiction books
- Novels, plays, poetry, and short stories

Quickly answer the following questions in your mind:

- How well do you comprehend what you read?
- How well do you remember what you read?
- What are your strong points as a reader?
- What is the one thing you would most like to change about the way you read?

Play with two possible scenarios for your future, based on how you read today.

Here is one we call the plight of the elementary reader:

You enter your office greeted by stacks of unread email, reports, manuals, and journals. Those piles of paper feel like a reprimand. Rather than face them, you stash them. But you cannot help worrying that you have buried a vital idea or fact—some critical insight that could lead to a promotion or help you avoid an embarrassing mistake. As you plod through your daily round of meetings and phone calls, you tell yourself that you will get to all that reading... tomorrow.

The situation at home is similar. Piles of untouched magazines, newspapers, and mail clutter your living space. The prospect of hacking your way through it seems distant, at best. How about your chance to read for pleasure—to enjoy those novels, biographies, and motivational books you have been saving for a special day? That day just keeps retreating behind everything else that comes along.

The idea of further professional training or education seems to make sense. You get excited thinking about the career advances and extra income that you stand to gain. A question that stops you cold: How would I ever get all that reading done?

Even if, by some miracle, you conquered all of those unread stacks, you still face the challenge of remembering, explaining, and applying what you read. So, you put off reading another day and live in a state of confusion, chaos, and quiet desperation.

Is this scenario familiar to you? Are you trying to cope in the information age using reading skills learned in elementary school?

Now consider scenario number two, which we will call the joy of the PhotoReader:

You begin each workday feeling on top of the information needed to make effective and timely decisions. Whenever you read, you do so with a sense of effortlessness and relaxation. You find it easier to win approval for your proposals because your recommendations are backed by solid evidence.

Reading technical reports, a task that used to consume hours, now requires only minutes per document. At the end of your day you look at a clear desk feeling ready for the following day.

This quality extends to your home life as well. Gone are the piles of untouched books, magazines, newspapers, and mail that once crowded your living space. You keep up with the latest daily news in 10 to 15 minutes a day. In a single sitting you pare down or eliminate your

"to be read" piles. And with the extra time, you consistently complete the top-priority tasks on your to-do lists.

Your advanced reading abilities enable you to take courses, complete degrees, gain promotions, learn new skills, expand your knowledge, and satisfy your general curiosity. The ease of it all makes learning fun.

Now you create time for novels, magazines, and pleasure reading that go beyond the immediate demands of your job. In the process, you create free time to play as well.

Hold this scenario in mind for a few more seconds. Savor the resulting feelings of mastery and pleasure. Enjoy the extra time, money, and pleasure that reading adds to your life. Isn't that empowering?

Decide your future now

One message I hope you will take from this book, above all others, is that you can choose which scenario is true for you. You can place yourself on a path to either of these worlds in a moment. You already possess the power to create either scenario, and it is imperative to decide and shape the future you want.

If this appeal to shape your destiny as a reader seems overly dramatic or silly, then consider a statistic: fewer than 10 percent of the people who buy a book ever get beyond the first chapter. (Congratulations! You are already into Chapter 2.)

Many people who enroll in our PhotoReading seminar say they typically never make it beyond the cover of the books they buy. Instead, they simply accumulate or circulate books, magazines, brochures, mail, email, and reports. The information in these materials could just as well be written in disappearing ink.

As you go beyond the opening of this book, you will discover a set of tools for gaining a new experience of reading. Use the tools, and you will find it within your power to make the ideal reading scenario come true for you. If you do not go beyond this chapter, your experience of reading will stay the same as it is today.

Break old reading habits

I know you want results, and you will probably try many of the techniques I suggest. However, achieving new results means more than trying new reading behaviors. You must adopt an alternative view of what reading can be.

Consider everything you know about reading and **you have just defined the barriers to getting new results.** Elementary school reading imprints us all with a model of reading that limits our minds. This model or "paradigm" exerts tremendous power over your actions and your potential results.

Elementary reading is a fairly passive affair, often done without a clear sense of purpose. Have you ever spent ten minutes reading a newspaper article to discover it was a waste of time? That happens when you read passively.

One-speed-fits-all is the elementary reading maxim; generally we plow through every type of reading material—from comic books to textbooks—at the same rate. It makes more sense to get the facts from a trade journal with a different speed than we would use reading a novel for pleasure.

We feel pressure to get it right the first time with elementary reading. We expect to comprehend everything in one pass through the material. If we do not, we feel inadequate as readers. Musicians do not pressure themselves to play music from a score perfectly the first time. Why must we be perfect as readers?

Think about all the tasks we are supposed to accomplish in that single pass through a document: comprehend the structure, grasp the key terms, and follow the main arguments or plot events. On top of that, we must remember it all, critique it, and quote it accurately.

Faced with these kinds of demands, the conscious mind often becomes overwhelmed and can literally shut down. This is compounded when we feel anxiety, which happens when we come to the end of a paragraph and have no idea what we just read. Has this happened to you?

Becoming overwhelmed by too much information is easy in this age of information overload. Have you ever found your eyes moving down the page while your mind went off to a far away land? It is as if the lights are on, but nobody is home.

This leads to document shock—a short circuit in your internal connections. Too much current coming over the lines sends the wiring up in smoke.

This breakdown at the conscious level slows the flow of information to a trickle when we read. The more facts, details, and other data we try to cram in, the less we recall.

In this age of information overload, it is easy to feel like a starving person with a can of soup but no can opener. With elementary reading skills, we often leave hungry. We plow through books, periodicals, manuals, and email, only to find that we are craving something we cannot seem to get. Anything useful from these piles of information remains sealed from us.

Will elementary reading habits deliver what we need? If your answer is "no," you know the problem exists—and that is great. You have entered a powerful place, one where you are poised for change.

Embrace new reading choices

Readers who thrive today take a different approach than the elementary school model of reading. They are flexible in their reading. They adjust their speed to the type of material at hand. They know what they want from the written piece. They consistently find gems of information that deliver real benefit.

Active, purposeful, questioning, and fully engaged—that describes the best readers. These effective reading strategies become a part of your repertoire as you learn the PhotoReading whole mind system. In the process, you will discover enhanced retention, recall, and enjoyment.

PhotoReading shifts you away from the prevailing elementary reading model into whole mind reading and makes you a blasphemer of traditional reading theory. As such you will encounter many people who will say PhotoReading cannot possibly work. The next story illustrates what I mean.

A colleague at Learning Strategies Corporation discovered that even college professors resist new paradigms. Faculty members at a college in Minnesota tried to block us from offering the PhotoReading seminar on the grounds that PhotoReading is impossible.

The PhotoReader agreed to offer a demonstration. A volume of U.S. patent law was projected, page by page, onto a video monitor. My colleague PhotoRead this material as it was displayed at approximately 30 pages a second (over 690,000 words a minute). Afterwards, he scored 75 percent comprehension. In addition, he drew approximations of six patent illustrations and correctly identified their numeric sequence.

The paradigm had shifted right before their eyes. Do you suppose they supported the seminar? No. Seeing is not believing. To shift your paradigm **you must believe it before you see it**. Think of

PhotoReading as a paradigm shift, and you will do the "impossible." With practice of the techniques described in this book, you can get to the same super fast speeds.

You cannot "read" at 25,000 words a minute

Before learning PhotoReading, many people hear such stories as above and respond with, "That is crazy! There is no way you can read that fast."

They are right. No one's "conscious mind" can read that fast. PhotoReading is not "reading" as we know it. This kind of information processing is possible only when we temporarily bypass the critical, logical, analytical mind. We do not PhotoRead with the conscious mind. Instead, we draw on vast layers of the mind that remain largely unused during conventional reading. This literally means using the brain in a new way.

We still have to face everyday reading challenges, so let us employ an approach to reading that uses the whole mind. From the dominant "left hemisphere" we draw upon the abilities to analyze, sequence information, and reason logically. From the nondominant "right hemisphere" we obtain the abilities to synthesize, comprehend, create internal images, and respond intuitively.

When you learn to mentally photograph a book at a rate of one page a second—about 25,000 words a minute—you are taking a new approach to processing information. At such rates, the old left-to-right, word-by-word, line-by-line method of elementary reading cannot operate. Instead, you meet the printed page using abilities ascribed to the nonconscious, nondominant regions of the brain.

After PhotoReading a book, the next step is to stimulate and activate your brain. This step of "activation," as we call it, lets you extract information you need from the book to accomplish your goals for reading.

Accepting that you can process the written word at a nonconscious level shifts the reading paradigm. Make this shift, and you can make your experience of reading powerful, effective, and easy. As a beginning PhotoReader, you can get through a book now in three hours with full comprehension that would have taken ten hours in the past.

Take an unexpected path to success

Some aspects of PhotoReading may seem whimsical at first. Instead of learning the expected techniques of speed reading, you learn about the tangerine technique, cocktail weenies, remembering your dreams, and other unusual processes. I purposefully guide you through experiences that you have not had, possibly do not want, and may not think you need.

Sound odd? It is no more odd than discovering the principles of physics by learning how to downhill ski. Why not do it that way? To help the paradigm shift, we must take an unusual, unexpected path. Otherwise, we tend to solve our reading problem in ways that fit our current view of the problem.

For example, when we have a lot to read, we tend to speed up—but our comprehension drops. We then slow down and overload the conscious mind. The net result is no increase in speed or comprehension but an enormous increase in internal conflict. This conflict recreates the problems we attempted to solve. And we still have a lot to read.

It takes away our excuses

If the thought of zipping through a book at a page a second sounds unlikely, remember that a new approach always seems outlandish when we view it through the lenses of the old model. When a paradigm shifts, everything begins again. Old rules may no longer apply. Even so, profound changes can happen painlessly, in an instant, and have far-reaching effects.

I like the way one of our PhotoReading graduates, a mechanical engineer, put it: "It is scary to think that our minds are unlimited. It takes away all our excuses." If you feel uneasy with the prospect of a paradigm shift, consider the words of another graduate: "Step into the unknown. Don't be afraid. You will either find solid ground, or you will be taught to fly."

We must try new attitudes and experiment with new actions. Otherwise, how can we produce new results in our lives? A person in one of our seminars overcame his fear of success and said, "I finally understand. This seminar can transform my life—but I have been acting as though I can do it without changing any of my beliefs or my behavior!"

What you have to give up

To master PhotoReading you must give up:

Read
Bullets

- Low self-esteem as a learner.
- Self-defeating habits like procrastination and self-doubt.
- Perfectionism, "all or none" thinking that dwells on failure rather than feedback and learning.
- Distrust in the nonconscious mind and intuitive abilities.
- The need to know everything right away.
- Performance anxiety.
- A stressful sense of urgency.

More than anything else, you must give up negative attitudes that get in the way of your success. For example, one participant in a PhotoReading seminar never considered himself much of a reader, and his belief became a personal barrier: "I just don't think I am going to be able to learn this." Another participant in the same seminar also claimed poor reading skills, but her approach was more open to giving up her limitations: "I am just going to do whatever it takes to master this."

Both people learned to PhotoRead. The first one, while clinging to a negative belief, found it much more difficult to discover the true abilities he possessed. When he made the important internal change, the PhotoReading whole mind system helped change his results in life.

As profound as PhotoReading can be to your life, there is an added reassurance: you do not have to give up any pleasure in reading. In fact, you get to keep your regular reading skills. A woman who loved reading novels exclaimed after taking PhotoReading, "I've rediscovered the joy of reading!" Her pleasure reading became a richer, fuller experience.

Here is the system

The demands placed on you as a reader in our age of information are tremendous. The PhotoReading whole mind system can help you meet any challenge. It works with any subject matter and flexibly adapts to different purposes, print formats, rates of speed, and levels of comprehension.

The five steps of the PhotoReading whole mind system use the abilities of your whole mind with power and effectiveness. Let us overview the steps now. In the next five chapters you will develop skills to apply each step effectively.

Step 1) Prepare

Read to
end of
Chapter

Reading effectively begins with a clear sense of *purpose*. This means consciously stating a desired outcome for reading. For example, you might want a brief overview of main points. You might want to gain certain details such as the solutions to specific problems. Perhaps you want to complete a task and seek only the ideas that will help you do so. Purpose acts like a radar signal to the inner mind allowing it to produce the results you seek.

Empowered with a clear purpose, you then enter a state of *relaxed alertness*—the ideal state of mind for reading and learning. While in this state, neither boredom nor anxiety exists. You are exerting effort, but you are not worried about results. Have you ever watched young children as they play? They model the same relaxed yet purposeful state we seek here.

Step 2) Preview

Previewing is based on an important principle: effective learning often takes place "from whole to parts." That is, you start with the big picture and proceed to the smaller, more detailed parts.

When done effectively, previewing is short and sweet—about 60 to 90 seconds for a book, 60 seconds for a long report, and as little as 30 seconds for a short article. During that time, you look over the material to get a general idea of what will be covered in the book or document, clarify and refine your purpose, and decide whether to continue reading or call it quits.

As children we are told, "Look before you leap." Previewing is like looking into a pool of water and dipping your toes in before jumping in to swim. It gives you a sense for the essence of the material and what you might expect to encounter, helping you determine whether you want to go further with the materials.

Step 3) PhotoRead

The PhotoReading technique begins with placing ourselves more fully into the relaxed, alert state of mind and body called the resource level of mind. In this state, distractions, worries, and tensions seem to fall away.

Then you adjust your vision for the *PhotoFocus* state. Here the aim is to use your eyes in a new way: instead of bringing individual words into sharp focus, you soften your eyes so that your peripheral vision expands and you see the four corners of the book.

PhotoFocus creates a physical and mental window—allowing direct exposure of the incoming visual stimuli to the brain. In this state, you mentally photograph the entire page, exposing it to the preconscious processor of the mind. The exposure of each page stimulates a direct neurological response. The brain performs its function of pattern recognition, unencumbered by the critical/logical thought process of the conscious mind.

At a rate of one page a second, you can PhotoRead a whole book in three to five minutes. This is not traditional reading. After PhotoReading, you may have little if any conscious awareness of the material, which means you may consciously know nothing. The next steps create the conscious awareness we need.

Step 4) Postview

After PhotoReading, you move directly into postviewing. During this step you create a plan for your later activation. The three quick parts of postviewing take only 12 minutes and include making an in-depth survey of the materials, locating "trigger words," and creating questions that you want answered.

Survey articles for a minute so that you can notice any interesting sections, graphs, tables, bold print that might relate to your purpose. When surveying a book, you might take two to three minutes. Surveying is like x-raying a book—getting a sense of its underlying structure. Structure gives  you something that learning theorists call a schema, a set of expectations about how an author presents his or her ideas. When you know the structure of written text, you become more accurate at predicting its content. As a result, your comprehension and reading pleasure soar.

Trigger words are the key words on a page that alert your mind to the details you might want to explore more thoroughly later on. Trigger words build curiosity and stimulate the brain to create associations and neural connections. Do not look at every page; one in every 20 pages works for finding these words. After you have found 10 to 20 trigger words, it is time to formulate questions that you want to answer about the text. Good questions lead to fast, effective activation.

Step 5) Activate

The first part of activation is easy; simply put the material aside for 20 minutes to 24 hours. During activation you restimulate the brain with questions you created during postview and start to explore parts of the text to which you feel most attracted.

You have a variety of activation tools to choose from depending on your purpose. For example, you can *super read* the most important parts of the text by scanning quickly down the center of each page or column of type. When you feel it is appropriate, *dip* into the text for more focused reading to comprehend the details. In dipping, you allow your intuition to say, "Hey, turn to the last paragraph on page 147! Yes, that is the one. The ideas you want are right there."

Other activation techniques developed while reading this book include *rhythmic perusal*, *skittering*, and *mind mapping*. These also help you gain access to the deeper impressions established by PhotoReading. When you read highly technical or complex material, you may choose an activation technique called *rapid reading*. It is also the activation of choice for reading novels.

In summary, when you activate, you involve your whole brain, connect the text with your conscious awareness, and achieve your goals for reading.

With this overview in mind, you are ready to do it.

A public relations specialist found himself in a toy store after learning to PhotoRead. He said, "I became very playful after learning PhotoReading."

An executive said that PhotoReading dozens of books on management principles has improved his job performance. Another received an unusually large pay raise a year after the PhotoReading class—she said she developed such an increased understanding of the industry through PhotoReading that it dramatically improved her productivity.

A salesperson from London PhotoRead a selection of books on self-esteem and confidence building because his sales were low. He noticed an immediate change in his confidence, attitude, and sales.

A graphic artist routinely PhotoRead design books. He said it heightened his creative ability.

A mother PhotoRead her children's homework to better help them with their studies.

A proofreader discovered that, after PhotoReading documents first, she missed fewer mistakes.

A 13-year-old PhotoRead his mom's college textbook hoping to help her with her homework. He immediately understood the problem. His mom then pledged to learn PhotoReading.

An amateur chef found himself creating delicious new recipes after PhotoReading his library of cookbooks.

A PhotoReader PhotoRead 23 books on Shakespeare over a several week period hoping to build a foundation so that he could appreciate Shakespeare. Then he sat back with one of Shakespeare's plays. For the first time in his life he understood why so many people have enjoyed Shakespeare's work. He found the play easier to read, fascinating, and enjoyable.

A new homeowner PhotoRead all the home-improvement books he could find. Friends who helped him on his projects were amazed at how much he knew and began calling him for advice.

A high school defensive football coach repeatedly PhotoRead football playbooks prior to the start of the season. He discovered during game situations he could predict the opposing team's offensive strategy and respond with the ideal defensive play. His thinking speed and mental alertness were dramatically improved.

A PhotoReader lost his job after learning PhotoReading. He credits his higher paying, new job to PhotoReading and learning a new industry quickly.

An entrepreneur had difficulty understanding the advice of his legal counsel. He PhotoRead several books on the subject in a bookstore. As he was leaving, a flash of insight streaked through his mind, drawing him back to the books. He intuitively grabbed one from the shelf, and opened the book automatically to the page that offered a clear explanation of the advice.

Part Two:

Learn the
PhotoReading
Whole Mind System

3

Step 1) Prepare

I perform better at any activity, from public speaking to fishing, if I am well prepared. Yet, I used to pick up a book or magazine and just start reading with no preparation at all.

Now I treat reading as a goal-oriented activity. Preparing for a few moments increases my concentration, comprehension, and retention of what I read. Preparing may seem simple, but it is the foundation of effective reading. All steps of the PhotoReading whole mind system actually revolve around preparation.

Being prepared to PhotoRead is much more than getting the book out to read it. It involves stating your purpose and fixing your point of attention to enter the ideal state of mind.

1) State your purpose

Establishing purpose is hardly a new idea. Francis Bacon, the sixteenth-century English philosopher, said it well, "Some books are to be tasted, others to be swallowed, and some few to be chewed and digested; that is, some books are to be read only in parts, others to be read but not curiously, and some few to be read wholly, and with diligence and attention."

All reading ultimately serves a purpose, either consciously or unconsciously. When you state your purpose explicitly, you greatly increase the odds of attaining it. Purpose unleashes ability. Almost anything can be accomplished with a strong sense of purpose. Purpose is the engine that drives the PhotoReading whole mind system.

Establishing purpose is power that can be felt emotionally and physically. Readers with a firm sense of purpose acquire new feelings about the act of reading. They sit as if they mean business. When you have strong purpose, your body becomes strong and alert.

Set your purpose by asking questions such as:

Read italics only

• *What is my ultimate application of this material?* What will I expect to do or say differently after reading it?

• *How important is this material to me?* In the long run, how worthwhile is it? Does reading this material create value for me? If so, what specifically is that value?

• *What level of detail do I want?* Do I want to emerge from reading it with the big picture? Do I want to understand only the main points? Do I want to recall specific facts and other details? Is reading the entire document relevant to my purpose? Could I gain what I want by reading a single chapter or section instead?

> Example of purpose: A human resource consultant went to the library to PhotoRead the corporate report on a prospective client before their initial meeting. Her purpose for the eight minutes she invested was to get a feel for the trends of the company, where they had come from, and where they were headed. Her goal was to get in sync with the corporate executives and relate her skills effectively to their present and future needs.
>
> Example of purpose: A banker wanted to interface his new computer with his new printer. After hours of trying, he remained unsuccessful. Before going to bed, he PhotoRead both manuals. His purpose was to let his nonconscious mind work out the details of the problem and solve it upon awakening. Within the first half-hour after awakening, he had the printer working perfectly.

• *How much time am I willing to commit right now to satisfy my purpose?* Making a time commitment gently forces attention on the task. I am increasing the importance of reading, because it is the only thing I choose to do right now.

In summary, do you want a general understanding of information, or do you need subtle details? Do you want to study something, or just gain pleasure and relaxation?

Too many people are on a trip with no destination. They approach reading with no sense of where they want to go. If I do not get value from what I am reading, I ask, "What is my purpose?" Invariably the answer is a resounding "Huh?" If I do not have purpose, my reading is passive and often wasteful.

Purpose and time management are inseparable. In the information age, you can no longer presume to read every document at the same speed or level of comprehension. Not only is this impossible given the amount of material you need to read, it is not even desirable. As Francis Bacon put it, some things are worth reading in great detail; others are not worth reading at all.

Keep in mind that your purpose can be quite inventive. For instance, your main purpose for reading in the dentist's office may be distraction: you simply want to avoid thinking about the sound of the drill in the next room. That is a legitimate purpose and prompts a distinctive experience of reading.

State your purpose every time you read. This habit engages the mind and increases concentration. When you establish your purpose, the full power of your mind comes into play.

In addition, purpose loosens the grip of guilt, a word that frequently arises when people talk about their reading habits. Many of us were imprinted with strict rules about how we were "supposed to read." One man said, "I bought the darn magazine, so even if I don't want to read all the articles, I am compelled to finish the whole thing."

With a sense of purpose, you can justify putting aside the material you do not need to read. Simply weed out the publications that fail to create value for you.

Establishing purpose takes as little as two seconds, yet the payoffs can save you hundreds of hours over the course of your lifetime. This technique is so far-reaching that it can instantly and permanently changes the effectiveness of your reading.

2) Enter the ideal state for reading

When I read most efficiently, my body is relaxed and my mind is alert. If I maintain relaxed alertness, I am more able to comprehend, retain, and recall what I read.

To help you quickly and easily establish the ideal state of relaxed alertness, you can use the "tangerine technique." This simple technique automatically directs your attention and immediately improves reading performance.

Studies show that both reading and memory require attention. You can consciously attend to seven, plus or minus two, different bits of information at one time. (That is why telephone companies originally made phone numbers seven digits long.) In other words, you have approximately seven units of attention available at any moment.

Research also indicates that fixing one unit of attention on a single point helps you effectively focus your other available units of attention when reading. Where you fix your point of attention is important. For example, when driving a car, the best point of attention is down the road—not on your hood ornament or the bumper on the car in front of you. For the efficient reader, the ideal point of attention is just behind and above the head.

The tangerine technique helps locate and maintain the ideal point of attention and instantly creates the relaxed, alert state of body and mind we desire for reading. Here are the steps to follow:

Read
Bullets

• Hold an imaginary tangerine in your hand. Experience the weight, color, texture, and smell of the tangerine. Now toss it into the other hand and catch it. Toss the tangerine back and forth between your hands.

• Now catch the tangerine in your dominant hand and bring it to the top back part of your head. Touch that area gently with your hand. Imagine feeling the tangerine resting there while you bring your arm down and relax your shoulders. You can pretend this is a magic tangerine, and it will stay in place no matter where you put it.

• Gently close your eyes and let the tangerine balance on the back of your head. Notice what happens to your physical and mental state as you do this. You will feel relaxed and alert. With your eyes closed, imagine your field of vision opening up.

• Maintain the relaxed feeling of alertness as you open your eyes and begin reading.

Here is an experiment you can do now to discover the potential effects of the tangerine technique. Take any page of this book you have not yet read. Without the tangerine in place, read two or three paragraphs. Afterwards, reflect on your experience. Then, put the tangerine in place, using the method described above, and read two or three new paragraphs. Compare your experiences.

During the experiment, you might be overly self-conscious of doing something different. If so, you might find the effect hard to detect. Many people report a wider visual field, fluid movement of the eyes with less staccato or jumpy movements, and the ability to read word phrases or even whole sentences at a glance. You might notice that you no longer need to reread sentences. You might even notice that the inner voice reading every word inside your head is quieting down.

Playing with this technique lets you flow through reading material with increased speed and ease. Your ability to concentrate on the information improves, and reading becomes more relaxing.

At first you will consciously place the tangerine on the back of your head. Soon it will become automatic so that, whenever you approach reading materials, one unit of attention fixes into place.

This physically relaxed and mentally alert state is also perfect for other important activities. It is widely researched as a state of peak human performance. This state is similar to contemplation, meditation, and prayer in which you are absorbed in the present moment.

While this is a state of relaxation, it is not the same as going to sleep or becoming drowsy. Rather, you focus your mind with an inner calmness. You have access to all your natural, inner resources.

Put it all together

The following procedure can help you prepare for reading in 30 seconds. You may wish to have a friend guide you through it or record it so that you can play it back later.

Read Bullets

• Place your reading materials in front of you. Do not read them yet.

• Begin to relax by closing your eyes. Become aware of yourself from head to toe. Your spine is erect, your posture is comfortable, and your breathing is relaxed.

• Mentally state your purpose for reading. (For example, "During the next ten minutes, I will read this magazine article for ideas to help me improve my time management skills.")

• Place the imaginary tangerine at the top back part of your head.

• Become aware of yourself as relaxed and alert. Bring a slight hint of a smile to the corners of your eyes and the corners of your mouth to relax your face. Even with your eyes closed, you can imagine your visual field opening up. You have a direct eye-mind connection.

• Now, at a rate that is comfortable for you, maintaining this state of relaxed alertness, gently open your eyes and begin reading.

More on the tangerine technique

The ideal state for reading is typically in short supply for many people, especially at work. When we read at work, the phone is often ringing, someone in the doorway is talking, we have to hurry to make a meeting, and extraneous thoughts about groceries or car repairs create a traffic jam in our heads. With such a morass of mental events, where does our attention end up? All over the place. Reading is next to impossible.

In contrast, the ideal state for reading is the flow state, when you are totally absorbed in the task at hand. That is where the tangerine technique comes into play.

In the mid 1980s, I read a fascinating article in *Brain/Mind Bulletin* about Ron Davis, a reading specialist. Davis had dyslexia, a reading disability. While searching for a solution to this problem, he made a discovery.

People with dyslexia, he found, have a roving point of attention, one that wanders through space without coming to a fixed point. Skilled readers, on the other hand, have a fixed point of attention located just behind and above the top of the head.

By training himself to redirect his attention, he raised his reading, writing, and spelling skills from an elementary to a college level in fewer than three years. Today, Davis runs a private clinic for people with learning disabilities. His excellent book, *The Gift of Dyslexia*, describes his method in detail. His sessions begin by training his clients to find the ideal point of attention, which he calls the "visuo-awareness epicenter."

I tried his technique myself and immediately noticed an increase in my concentration and ease in reading. If this technique had worked on dyslexics, I speculated, what might the effect be on a normal adult reader who has been too scattered to read efficiently.

Davis's work had provided me with a creative leap. To accomplish the effect of his "visuo-awareness epicenter," I developed the tangerine technique.

Most people find that several benefits flow immediately from the tangerine technique. To begin, they quickly and easily enter a relaxed state of alertness. In addition, they calm their minds and automatically focus their attention. The result is an instant improvement in reading skills.

Historically, the tangerine technique has come down to us in a variety of forms. The Chinese thinking cap, the wizard's cap, and even the original concept for the "Dunce cap," believe it or not, were all devices for focusing attention. Each causes part of your attention to fixate at a place above and behind your head.

Experiment with this technique. If the image of a tangerine does not seem to work for you, then try another way of fixing your attention to the place above and behind your head. You might snap your fingers behind your head if your brain likes auditory stimulation. Or, imagine wearing a sombrero, with a bird sitting on top of it. Feel the sombrero resting on your head and focus your attention on the bird.

Another way is to imagine standing outside of your body, looking over the top of your head, as you read. As you do this, notice the shift in the way you feel.

When you fix your point of attention with any of these techniques and open your eyes, a curious thing happens. Suddenly, the material you are reading seems more manageable. In this state, you are prepared to take in far more visual information than before.

Adjusting your state of mind is the goal. You are not trying to hold the feeling of a tangerine the entire time you read. Getting a fixed point of attention is much like setting a keystone at the top of a stone archway. The one stone at the top holds all the rest of the stones in place.

Similarly, the one fixed point of attention seems to gather and focus the other units of attention to the task of reading. Once you have placed it there, forget about it. When you pass through a doorway, you do not have to carry the doorway with you. Just go ahead and begin your reading—your mind will take care of the rest.

Take a moment to think of how you can use what you have learned in this chapter:

• Preparing is the foundation to the whole mind system.

• The two components to preparing are stating your purpose and getting into the ideal state of mind with a fixed point of attention at the top, back part of your head.

Read Bullets

• Reading purposefully means reading with power.

• The tangerine technique is one way to focus your attention that automatically leads to the ideal state of mind.

Give yourself a few moments now to apply this technique to the remaining chapters of this book. Visualize yourself reading the rest of this book with strong purpose. Imagine shifting your attention to a point just behind you and on top of your head. Again, notice the shift in your physical state when you do so. As you read, you feel more relaxed, centered, attentive, and fully absorbed. Now you are poised at the flow state, ready to learn.

Several PhotoReaders with strong eyeglass prescriptions have reported a shift in their vision impairment. Within a year of PhotoReading regularly, their annual eye exams did not follow the usual course of increasing prescription intensity. In fact, they reported a reversal to a lesser prescription. In each case, the optometrists claimed such reversals were extremely rare.

A 17-year-old high school student disliked reading. Now she reads more than ever before. "It's turned my life around."

A certified public accountant was asked to serve on a panel of business professionals discussing raising venture capital. Her hectic schedule left only an afternoon for preparation. She selected several books to PhotoRead and activate. She felt as well prepared as if she had spent several days reading and writing. She presented the information concisely, and it was well received.

A young student who was given the PhotoReading program as a gift joyfully expressed her thanks. "It was a great honor to learn this skill." It is a skill she plans to use for the rest of her life. She has seen improvement in her reading, studying, and test-taking abilities, and she hopes to cut her time spent on homework by half and still receive the good grades she's already getting. PhotoReading also has been a great relief to her 9th grade brother who was a slow reader. Faced with rigorous coursework he no longer anticipates late night studying sessions. "This program is a miracle worker. I can read through books in one night, compared to in a month, and still have almost complete comprehension! I will never read the same again."

4

Step 2) Preview

The more you know about a text before you read it, the easier it will be to read and understand.

You can only read what you already know. The human brain can only comprehend patterns that are familiar. Previewing provides the fast track to discovering these patterns. It accelerates your understanding of the material and can be accomplished in a minute or less. There are three stages to previewing:

1) Look over the material

2) Appraise the value for your purpose

3) Determine to go or not go further

1) Look over the material

When my wife and I considered purchasing our home, we first explored the neighborhood. We walked to the lakefront and around the block. We drove to the school and into town. We looked at a map and explored the nearby parks. In other words, we looked over the territory.

As you consider reading a book, the first thing you want to do is look at the organization or structure of the book. The author generally tells you what the book is going to cover in the table of contents.

You may be amazed at how much you can gain through this simple strategy. In some cases, you will find everything you want to know—just by understanding how the author arranges his or her ideas in the table of contents.

By going through the table of contents, you can often know what the text seems to be about and can predict what to expect. It can help direct you where to look for important information.

"How to" books, for example, usually present you with a number of tasks to perform in a certain order. A "what is" book often presents a problem and offers a solution. Most normal-sized books can be previewed in a minute or less. Occasionally, large textbooks or computer manuals may take an extra minute in order to understand their structure.

Looking over articles or reports, whether printed or electronic, requires a different approach since few provide a table of contents. For these, quickly scan the pages noticing titles, subtitles, bold type, and the first and last paragraphs. If you find yourself immersed in a section, simply remind yourself that this is not your purpose now. You only want the structure or organization the author has set down. You want to keep this step superficial.

Previewing has an added advantage of promoting long-term memory. Because it helps you categorize the material you read, you can build stronger associations to new information, resulting in better memory.

2) Appraise the value for your purpose

If you followed my advice from the previous chapter, you would have decided on a purpose for reading the book, report, or article when you chose to take a closer look at it. Now it is time for you to step back a moment and ask yourself whether this material is right for you, right for the purpose you had originally set. You have more information now. The new information helps you make important decisions. Does this book have information that is relevant to your purpose? Will reading this material further enrich or benefit your purpose in some way? When you preview, you get an idea as to whether the material is sufficient to meet your needs or whether you need to look elsewhere for what you seek.

There is an explosion of information coming out every day in print and electronic files—in books, articles, reports, newsletters, web pages, blogs, forums, and emails. Unless you learn to discern quickly which ones will serve you best, you can become bogged down reading words that contribute little or nothing to your purpose.

3) Determine to go or not go further

This leads you to the last part of previewing. It is decision time. Determine whether you want to go further with the document to extract more of its content. Think about whether you can meet your purpose for reading or whether you need to redefine that purpose. Remember the 80/20 rule? Ask yourself whether this book or article relates to your "top 20 percent."

> The 80/20 Rule: If all items are arranged in order of value, 80 percent of the value would come from only 20 percent of the items. The remaining 80 percent of the items would only contain 20 percent of the value.

You might decide not to read the document. That is one of the kindest things you can do for yourself in this age of information overload. Save yourself the trouble of ingesting information you do not want or need. You might decide you only need to know the document in a general way. Later, if you want more specific information, you will know where to find it. It is like using a set of encyclopedias: you do not have to read the contents of each volume. You only need to know enough to pull the correct volume off the shelf.

Always preview

I recommend the preview step before PhotoReading because it performs an important role, one that reading specialists call "an advance organizer." Previewing helps your brain identify categories for the upcoming information, like preparing file cabinets into which you will sort the incoming data. Any material you actively organize will be remembered longer just as any document properly filed could be easily retrieved. This is an important step in the PhotoReading system.

Children should learn to preview for its value in directing the novice mind. It ensures that the material going in with PhotoReading will be in the reader's best interests. The skilled PhotoReader almost never takes more than one to two minutes to determine whether they want to go further with a written document.

In summary

To make the technique of previewing easier to use on a consistent basis, take a moment right now to imagine the types of reading materials you might face in the coming week. Imagine previewing those various sources of information. Imagine how a few moments of previewing can save you hours of time this week alone. *Quickly tune into information you want and eliminate redundant and unnecessary reading.*

Chapter 5 brings you to the next step, PhotoReading, the most provocative and exciting step of all.

A businessman was asked to speak at a conference. He was unable to prepare for the presentation in the traditional sense of reading books, taking notes, and writing his speech. He was only able to PhotoRead several books, so he figured he could wing it. To his surprise his presentation flowed with aplomb. He even presented statistics that just popped into his head—apparently provided by his mind. He received excellent feedback from his audience and later verified every fact was in the books.

A computer programmer learned that by PhotoReading pages of code he quickly discovered program bugs. Another programmer said his ability to write effective code improved when he PhotoRead pages of code written by other programmers.

A father of two who works full time and whose wife holds a heavy graduate school course load decided to take two graduate-level business classes himself. He earned Bs in both courses, even though he spent only 30 to 45 minutes a week PhotoReading for a total of about 10 to 12 hours for the entire semester. During his sessions he would free-note answers to some questions, mind map others, or mind map an entire book for more detail. He was surprised to find that after PhotoReading he could even talk out loud to himself and hear the answers to his questions flowing out in his own words. "I will never ever go back to regular reading. This system works, period!"

5

Step 3) PhotoRead

PhotoReading rockets you to success at the speed of light. In today's information deluge, why drown with regular reading or barely survive with speed reading? Now you can thrive and succeed with PhotoReading. This chapter describes how to start using the most provocative step of the PhotoReading whole mind system. To master PhotoReading, keep a playful and open-minded attitude.

PhotoReading relies on the brain's natural ability to process information at a preconscious level. For those who let go and trust their mind to do the work, PhotoReading provides a phenomenal opportunity to discover their true potential for learning.

Through PhotoReading, you expose your brain to patterns of text by mentally photographing the printed page. This is not a technique to work hard at nor is it something that the conscious mind has to figure out in order to perform it better. To strain at practicing and perfecting it may be counterproductive. Use it and explore the results.

During the next few pages you will learn the ways to perform each step of the PhotoReading process. After learning them, play with PhotoReading this book.

1) *Prepare to PhotoRead*

Preparing yourself for PhotoReading is a matter of making a few decisions. What is it you want to PhotoRead? Place your reading material in front of you and ask yourself if you can spare the few minutes required to PhotoRead it.

Why do you want to take the time to PhotoRead this material? Clearly state to yourself what you expect to get from the materials. This act of establishing your purpose will be repeated more precisely later in the process. Purpose is essential.

Choose to remain attentive to this experience and let go of any outside interferences. Be in an open posture, comfortable, upright, relaxed, and ready to enter the accelerative learning state.

2) *Enter the resource level of mind*

Earlier in the PhotoReading whole mind system, you entered a state of relaxed alertness before previewing. Your aim now is to experience a similar, but more receptive, brain state—a state in which you have access to expanded capabilities of mind and increased readiness to learn.

Here is a procedure for entering this state, also called the resource level of mind. At first, this procedure might take several minutes to complete. Eventually, however, you will reach the desired state in the time it takes for one deep inhale followed by a gentle exhale.

• Make yourself comfortable. When you are first learning this technique, lie down. After that, sit back comfortably in a chair.

• Take in a deep breath. Exhale, and then close your eyes.

• Experience full physical relaxation. Take in a deep breath and hold it for a moment. As you exhale slowly, think of the number "3" and mentally repeat the word *Relax*. This is your physical relaxation signal. Then progressively relax the major muscle groups of your body from head to toe. Imagine a wave of relaxation flowing throughout your entire body. Let each muscle melt until it is pleasantly relaxed and free from tension.

• Now calm your mind. Take in a deep breath and hold it for a moment. Exhale slowly. Think of the number "2" and mentally repeat the word *Relax*. This is your mental relaxation signal. Let go of thoughts about the past or future. Focus your awareness on the present moment. As you breathe out, let any tensions, anxieties, or problems float away. As you breathe in, let peace and tranquility flow into every part of you.

• Take in another deep breath and hold it for a moment. Slowly exhale; mentally hear the sound of the number "1." As you do so, picture a beautiful flower in your mind's eye. This signals that you have focused your awareness and entered the resource level of mind—a state of expanded creativity and ability to learn.

Imagine yourself in a beautiful, quiet place. Become aware of the soothing sights, sounds, and feelings you experience there. Let yourself rest comfortably there for a few moments.

Before you proceed to the next steps, gently remind yourself to release any remaining tension or distractions. Remind yourself to maintain this state of physical and mental relaxation as you PhotoRead.

The above process of entering the resource level of mind allows you to establish contact with your nonconscious resources of mind. Entering this physical and mental state allows you to be more responsive to your own positive ideas. While in this highly attuned state, you open up access to the deeper "data base" of your long-term memory.

Brain states are characterized by subjective experiences and electroencephalograph (EEG) frequency measures (Hz stands for Hertz or cycles per second).
• Waking state = 12-23 Hz, Beta.
• Relaxed alertness, optimal for learning = 8-12 Hz, Alpha.
• Deeply relaxed, good for internal imagery, associated with creativity = 4-8 Hz, Theta.

Many classes, books, and CDs on relaxation and meditation can help you gain skill at entering the ideal learning state. The Learning Strategies Corporation Paraliminal CDs guide you through similar relaxation techniques used in PhotoReading seminars.

3) Affirm your concentration, impact, and purpose

Thoughts either support or derail the learning process. Positive, affirmative thoughts assist learning, and negative thoughts negate or prevent it.

Placing positive thoughts in your mind can help you develop skills and achieve desired results. These thoughts, called affirmations, help direct the material you PhotoRead to your inner mind. The most useful affirmations for PhotoReading include:

Read
Bullets

- "As I PhotoRead, my concentration is absolute."

- "All that I PhotoRead makes a lasting impression on my inner mind and is available to me."

- "I desire the information in this book, (say the title here), to accomplish my purpose of (restate your purpose)."

Affirmations give direction to your brain by clearly establishing goals. The process of affirming also bypasses the limitations imposed by the conscious mind. It redirects any negative internal dialog and opens you to the possibility of success.

It is important that your goal or purpose be one you can achieve. A poorly formed goal would be: "I want to have photographic recall of everything I PhotoRead." Since that is not the purpose of the PhotoReading step and perfect recall of everything is not reasonable, such an ill-formed goal could lead to undue frustration and nonperformance.

A well-formed goal would be: "I desire to fully absorb this material and to speed my application of these techniques and concepts in my life." The achievement of such a goal is within your control and leads to greater ease and success.

4) Enter the PhotoFocus state

The PhotoFocus state uses your sense of sight to input visual information directly into the nonconscious mind. In this step, you learn to use your visual system differently than with regular reading. Rather than hard focusing on individual words and word groups, you achieve a "soft gaze" to notice the entire page at once.

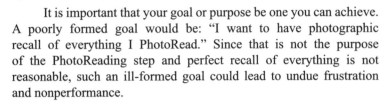

When I first developed PhotoReading, I knew that hard focusing the eyes sent information through the conscious mind. PhotoReading required sending information through the preconscious processor into the brain. My question became "How can I look at something without using hard focus to look at it?"

> You strengthen the eye-mind connection with PhotoFocus. This shifts the emphasis of reading away from the page in front of your eyes to its meaning which is stored behind your eyes (in your mind).

De-focusing the eyes was not the answer. That only made me feel spacey and lethargic. My feelings of relaxed alertness vanished as if my physical and mental clarity was connected to my visual clarity.

One afternoon I mulled over this paradox. I read an article about an art teacher named Betty Edwards. In her book *Drawing on the Right Side of the Brain*, she said, "If you want to draw my thumb, don't draw my thumb," because you will use the left brain—the analytical, non-artistic side of the brain. She said, "To draw my thumb, draw the space around my thumb." That strategy uses the right brain—the creative side of the brain.

Using her advice, I began looking at the two pages of an open book. I took in all the white space in one expansive gaze, not looking at the words. Suddenly, the pages took on a clarity and depth, appearing almost three-dimensional. In the center of the page there emerged a third, rounded narrow page.

This reminded me of experiences I had as a child. My mind tended to wander if I had to sit and wait. Occasionally, if I happened to be sitting in a room with a tile floor, I became aware that the floor appeared as a three-dimensional grid—as if there were two layers of lines, about six inches deep. If I tried to look at it, it would disappear. The effect would only linger if I maintained a relaxed, divergent gaze, as if looking into the distance.

The recognition of this unique visual state was the beginning of PhotoFocus. In the years since then, many discoveries have connected PhotoFocus to ancient traditions of seeing with the whole brain rather than the limited conscious mind.

The essence of PhotoFocus is using your eyes in a new way that is called "seeing with soft eyes." This contrasts with hard focus, which is the normal practice of getting a sharp, clear image of a single word, phrase, or line of print. With PhotoFocus, you open up your peripheral vision and prepare to mentally photograph entire pages at once. In so doing, you process visual information at a preconscious level and feed it directly into your brain's nonconscious memory storage system.

Seeing with "soft eyes" is hardly new. Taoist literature from China refers to an "all-seeing gaze." So does Carlos Casteneda, author of a popular series of books about the practices of Don Juan, a Mexican shaman.

A clear description of soft eyes comes from Miyamoto Musashi, a legendary fifteenth-century swordsman and author of *The Book of Five Rings*. In the book, Musashi refers to two types of vision. One he calls *ken*, an observation of surface appearance and external movement. *Kan*, in contrast, is seeing into the essence of things. Using the peripheral vision of kan, said Musashi, a warrior could spot an enemy and detect an impending attack before it happened. Though we have no enemies to attack, with PhotoReading we can use the other benefits of kan: calmness, concentration, creativity, intuition, and the ability to greatly expand our visual field.

The physiology behind kan—or PhotoFocus, as we call it—is fascinating. The retinas of our eyes can be divided into two regions. One is the fovea, which is densely packed with cells called cones. These cells bring images into hard focus. Each cone has a single nerve connecting it to the brain. Information entering the fovea is processed by the conscious mind.

As we move into the periphery of the retina, the second area, we find different cells called rods. Even though several hundred rods are connected to the same nerve, these cells are extremely sensitive. In fact, they can detect the light of a single candle ten miles away. While in the PhotoFocus state, we are drawing much more upon rod vision than cone vision. The periphery of our visual field is processed nonconsciously.

Using PhotoFocus, you reduce interference from the conscious mind. This interference includes "perceptual defenses" that filter incoming information. Reducing this interference will help you gain more of your brain's expansive processing capability.

Interference also produces the common phenomenon of tunnel vision. It can happen when you are looking for something in the kitchen, for example. It may be right there in front of you, but you do not see it because you are expecting it to be in a drawer, not on the counter. PhotoFocus trains your brain to open up and perceive more of the information available to you.

As a preparation for entering the PhotoFocus state, play with the following exercise. The aim is to experience a visual phenomenon I call the "cocktail weenie effect."

To see the cocktail weenie effect, find a spot on the wall to look at. Now, while continuing to look at the spot, hold your hands about 18 inches in front of your eyes. Then bring the tips of your index fingers together.

As you gaze at the spot just above the top of your index fingers, notice in your visual field what is happening to your index fingers. Keep your eyes relaxed and do not worry about bringing anything into sharp focus.

You may notice a ghost image that looks like a third finger, as in the following diagram:

That ghost image looks like a cocktail weenie.

This might seem like child's play, but in reality it signals a significant change in your vision. Seeing the cocktail weenie demonstrates you are diverging your eyes instead of converging them on a fixed point of hard focus. When you do this, your visual field softens, and your peripheral awareness expands. It is strange that you will see the effect only when you do not look directly at your fingers. I am asking you to see it without looking at it. That sounds like something a Zen master would say.

You can apply the same effect to the pages of a book. To experience this, fix your gaze on a point comfortably beyond the top of the book. Notice the four edges of the book and the white space between the paragraphs while gazing just over the top of the book at your spot on the wall. Because your eyes are diverging, you will see a doubling of the crease between the left-hand and right-hand pages. Begin to notice a little rounded strip of a phantom page (cocktail weenie page) between the crease lines. I call that page the "blip page."

See if you can move your gaze down from over the top of the book, so that you are looking right through the center of the book as if you had x-ray vision. Can you maintain divergent eyes and still notice the blip page?

In the early stages of learning PhotoFocus, many people discover that their eyes try to focus on the book. This causes the crease lines to converge, and the blip to disappear. That is the power of habit. Do not fight it. Just relax and play with it. You may want to leave it and play with it again later.

When in PhotoFocus, the print on the page is probably blurred. That is okay, because to see the blip, you must place your focal plane at some distance away. To have clarity up close, you will need to relax your eyes and have the focal plane move in.

When you develop PhotoFocus, there is a unique clarity and depth to the words on the page. They are not in focus, because you are not looking at them. But, there is a clarity to the print that you can notice as you relax more.

Here is another way to see the blip page. Sit back from a table just a bit. Place your open book on the table near the edge. Look past the bottom edge of the book and see your feet on the floor. Slowly move the book into your visual field so that it almost covers your line of sight to your feet. If you notice the book in your visual field, you will probably realize that there is a doubling of the crease in the book. Between the two crease lines, something appears. That is the blip page.

Play with moving yourself more toward the book (and the book more toward you) until your line of sight is right through the center of the book, and you still have the double line. Can you do it? If it is tough, do not worry. After years of habitually focusing on the printed page, your first exposure to PhotoFocus might be challenging. Then again, you might find this to be easy.

No blip? No problem! If you do not see the blip page, you can still be a proficient PhotoReader. Remember, the goal of PhotoFocus is to minimize conscious processing and maximize preconscious processing. Seeing the blip page signals you have a divergent gaze, which is one way of preventing conscious processing. But there is another way:

Looking at an open book—right at the center crease—open up your field of vision so that you see all four corners of the book. Soften your gaze so that the lines of print are not in hard focus. Notice the empty margins and the white space between paragraphs. Imagine an "X" connecting the four corners of the book. (Use this technique if you are sighted in only one eye.)

As you experiment with these techniques, go easy. Remember, hard work does not help. Relaxing and noticing your experience are the main ingredients of success. After playing with your visual system for two or three minutes, just close your eyes and rest for a few minutes before you play again.

Many of these exercises can help strengthen and balance your visual system. Since all natural eye improvement methods are based on relaxation, it is important to give yourself the chance to rest your eyes.

The point of these exercises is not to hallucinate but to teach yourself how to diverge your eyes. Achieving "soft eyes" and maintaining PhotoFocus while PhotoReading will take time, so be patient.

The ideal posture for PhotoReading is sitting upright, with the book propped up at a 45 degree angle to the table (90 degrees to your eyes). If you tuck your chin in slightly you straighten your spine, permitting better energy flow to your brain. Your gaze will be through the center of the book, but at first, it is okay if you gaze over the top in order to see the blip. If you cannot maintain the blip at first, simply notice the four corners and the "X," rather than struggle with divergence.

5) Maintain a steady state while flipping pages

Your resource level of mind and PhotoFocus state may be fragile at first. Distracting and self-critical thoughts may disrupt your attention, and you might find yourself tempted to bring the printed page into hard focus again. If this happens, simply remind yourself that your purpose right now is to maintain an ideal state for learning. Place the imaginary tangerine on the back of your head (refer back to Chapter 3), and notice the blip page again.

You can use two additional techniques to maintain your state while PhotoReading. First, keep your breathing deep and even. Second, chant to the rhythm of the turning pages. These actions occupy your conscious mind, keeping it free from distractions while your nonconscious mind continues PhotoReading. The chant—a rhythmic internal statement of supportive words—is particularly important, because it focuses your mind and blocks negative thoughts that might otherwise occur.

Maintaining a steady state will enable you to breeze through books quickly and effectively. The steady rhythm is wonderful for keeping the brain relaxed and open while you mentally photograph the pages.

Here is how to maintain the resource level of mind while PhotoReading:

Read Bullets

• Remain in an open posture. Rest your feet on the floor with your legs uncrossed.

• Keep your breathing deep and even.

• Turn the pages of the book in a steady rhythm—one page every second or two. See every two-page spread with "soft eyes." Your gaze is through the center of the book, noticing the blip page. If you cannot see the blip, notice the four corners of the book, the white space on the pages, and an imaginary "X" connecting the four corners.

• Chant to the rhythm of your turning pages. Take one flip for each syllable of the following chant as you mentally repeat:

Re-lax…Re-lax…

Four-Three-Two-One…

Re-lax…Re-lax…

Keep the state…See the page…

• Do not concern yourself with missing pages. Just let them go. You can always come back to them on a second pass through the book.

• Continue the chant to the rhythm of your page turning. Let your conscious mind follow the words of the chant.

• Let go of distracting thoughts by bringing your conscious mind gently back to the activity at hand.

6) Close the process with a sense of mastery

The conscious mind has a natural tendency to question what it gains from PhotoReading. If you tell someone you just PhotoRead a book in three minutes, the first question asked is "What can you tell me about it?" Comedian Woody Allen joked about speed reading, "I just read *War and Peace*. It's about Russia."

Such a statement simply indicates that you receive little or nothing at a conscious level while PhotoReading, which is largely true. Unfortunately, it also implies that nothing was gained at a deeper, nonconscious level. This easily becomes a negative, self-fulfilling prophecy. Statements such as "I won't remember a thing" or "This can't possibly work" act like commands to your brain to forget what it gained while PhotoReading. If you continually make such statements, you will find that they become fulfilled.

PhotoReading downloads information directly onto the neural networks of your brain, which immediately begins processing it, spontaneously, at a level below the threshold of conscious awareness. To ensure your brain will have access to information you PhotoRead, close your PhotoReading session by taking charge of your thoughts and setting the stage for activation. Now is the time to request that your mind integrate the information and make it available for future use.

You instruct your brain on what to do with that information using affirmations. Affirmations that we use in our seminars include:

• I acknowledge the feelings I have received from this book, and…

• I release this information for my body and mind to process.

• I am curious as to how many ways my mind and body can demonstrate that this information is available to me.

Your response to the material you PhotoRead occurs within you. These affirmations invite your nonconscious mind to help. It is fun to consciously recognize the many ways this information can become available.

If you like, you can imagine a bridge between your conscious and inner mind along which the information flows. As you let go and relax even more, you can more easily notice whatever flows into your conscious awareness.

The six steps of the basic PhotoReading procedure are easy to put together. Do not let their simplicity deceive you. This technique can have a profound impact on you.

Consider PhotoReading before sleep

With PhotoReading, you blast information through your nervous system in a powerful way—like drinking water through a fire hose. Be open, let it digest and absorb at a nonconscious level. To do so, relax and let go.

The mind reviews information during the sleep state that has been taken in below the conscious level of awareness. Studies dating back to the early 1900s show that such information can have quite an effect on one's dreams. Since this is going to happen, you may as well make sure you PhotoRead books that are emotionally gentle and comforting before going to sleep.

You now have learned the six steps to the PhotoReading process. In order they are:

Read
Numbers

1) Prepare to PhotoRead.

2) Enter the resource level of mind.

3) Affirm your concentration, impact, and purpose.

4) Enter the PhotoFocus state.

5) Maintain a steady state while flipping pages

6) Close the process with a sense of mastery.

If you have not tried it yet, take a few minutes to PhotoRead this book, or, before you go to sleep tonight, PhotoRead another positive and uplifting book.

After you have prepared, previewed, and PhotoRead, you are ready to bring the knowledge you desire into your conscious awareness as you learn to activate in Chapter 6.

A student used PhotoReading to mind map the subject matter of his science exam, a nine-week comprehensive final. He missed only one question, but because he answered a bonus question, he scored 100 percent. Typically he never scored much beyond the 80s or low 90s on his exams, so he was very excited.

6

Step 4) Postview

After PhotoReading you have information in your nonconscious mind that you may want to know consciously. Postviewing takes advantage of the human brain's ability to classify perceptions and recognize patterns. Without these classifications and patterns the text would appear as the world does to a newborn—a constant parade of unrelated sights, sounds, and other sensations, a "blooming, buzzing confusion," as the father of psychology, William James, described it.

Postviewing allows you to build meaningful categories, recognize patterns, and locate the core concepts that lead to understanding. You start to discover the 4 to 11 percent of the text that includes its key message and satisfies your purpose. Postviewing gives you the opportunity to playfully begin your activation of the material.

You can begin postviewing right after the PhotoReading session, or you can wait a day or so. If you wait, I recommend PhotoReading the materials again, which will take only a few minutes.

The steps to postviewing are:

1) Survey the material

2) Find trigger words

3) Formulate questions

1) Survey the material

In addition to looking over the table of contents of a book or the titles and bold type of articles, you now have a chance to explore the structure of the material in greater depth by looking at:

Read
Bullets

• Text on the front and back covers

• Copyright date

(In some instances you will want to review the cover text and copyright dates during the initial preview, especially when timeliness is an issue.)

• Index

• First and last pages of a book or first and last paragraphs in shorter documents

• Text printed in bold or italic type including headings and subheadings

• Material set off as boxes, figures, charts, or graphics

• Previews, summaries, or reviews

The survey gives you an opportunity to see if the organization of the book will serve your purpose.

2) Find trigger words

Have you ever felt while reading that certain words leapt off the page, begging for special attention? Chances are those words focus the points of the author's message. Those words have an urgency. "Hey, look at me," they seem to say. Those words are *trigger* words.

Trigger words are key words—the high visibility, repeatedly used terms—central to the book. They are the handles to help you grasp the meaning of a text.

Finding trigger words helps the conscious mind formulate questions for the nonconscious mind to answer. Your brain highlights them in its search through the text, helping you quickly find meaning that accomplishes your purpose.

Locating trigger words is simple. For example, in Chapter 2 of this book, I mention elementary reading, paradigm shift, purpose, and beliefs. Those terms qualify as trigger words, because spotting them helps you develop curiosity, an essential ingredient in effective learning and efficient reading.

Most people locate trigger words with ease when it comes to nonfiction. When postviewing fiction such as short stories, plays, novels, and poetry you will see trigger words in the names of persons, places, and things.

Locating trigger words is a fun way to test the waters before diving for meaning. Try it. Glance down the text of a page every 20 pages or so as you flip through this book and notice what words catch your attention.

All places you survey will aid your search: book covers, table of contents, headings, and the index. In an index, for example, look for the words that are followed by the most page numbers. These are bound to be important trigger words.

Write a list of 20 to 25 trigger words for books and make a mental note of 5 to 10 trigger words for an article. You should be able to reach those numbers in two minutes or less.

Be playful and relaxed, and you will find it easier to spot high-powered terms.

3) Formulate questions

The human brain has a remarkable ability to search for and find answers to questions. With that in mind, use trigger words to stimulate questions you want answered during activation. When you look over your list of trigger words, perhaps only a few of them will result in questions that have value to you. The key is to arouse curiosity about material, which helps you become an active, questioning, purposeful, and powerful reader. Write any questions down, because they will be useful when you activate the material.

The secret to successful postviewing is to avoid getting into a text too deeply too soon. You may find yourself tempted to stop postviewing and start reading for answers to the questions. Notice your urge to focus on the particulars, let that urge go, and return to creating more questions. The brain needs time to incubate and integrate the information you have just PhotoRead.

You want to get the maximum benefit from every minute you invest in reading. If you start reading for details too soon, you could easily end up slowing down, plodding through paragraphs and pages that have no relevance to your purpose. That could lead to the loss of momentum, waning interest, and even a wonderful nap.

To avoid this, hold back from diving into the details. This strengthens your motivation. It creates a desire in you to find out more, to fill in the general structure that you are building in your mind.

One of the richest rewards of postviewing is getting hungry for information and ideas. That hunger increases your commitment to reading and energizes the whole mind to achieve your desires.

Now we are ready to find the answers to those questions through various activation techniques.

A PhotoReader was giving a radio interview about PhotoReading. She PhotoRead a book by an author who had just been interviewed. The author asked her specific questions about the book, and the PhotoReader spoke in great detail precisely answering the questions.

On another radio show, the astounded host exclaimed after hearing the PhotoReader's answer to a question, "You are almost rereading this page. That is page 97 randomly pulled out of the book. That's exactly what it says there." Later in the show he said, "It sounds like I have the author on."

A man in his thirties with a neurological disorder PhotoRead books at the university's medical library hoping to find clues. He later woke from a nap with an unusual dream regarding the disorder. He called his doctor who said, "I hadn't considered that. Let me consult a colleague."

An attorney found himself challenging an expert witness during cross-examination without a clear sense of why he was asking the questions. It became obvious as the testimony of the expert witness unraveled. The evening prior the attorney had PhotoRead books that contained facts contradicting those of the witness. At a conscious level, the attorney did not know the facts. From a nonconscious level, his mind had given him the guidance necessary to achieve his goal.

7

Step 5) Activate

A professor at a Minnesota university had been asked to give a speech. Most of what he wanted to present was contained in two books, so he PhotoRead them at bedtime, expecting to activate them the next day.

That night he dreamed of delivering his speech. He awoke from his dream, grabbed a pencil and paper, and jotted down everything he could remember of his dream/speech.

In the morning he reviewed his dream notes and realized his speech was completed, save a few transitions. Later that day he examined the books and discovered his notes contained all of the relevant points he needed.

I love hearing such stories from PhotoReaders. Those examples are great when they happen. For beginning PhotoReaders those experiences are the exception rather than the rule. This chapter explores how to consciously access information you need from materials you PhotoRead. I do not advocate merely sitting back and hoping to dream about information, expecting to be ready to speak before a group or perform on a school test. Actively engaging information makes comprehension occur.

Activation, the final step in the PhotoReading whole mind system, gives you the conscious awareness needed to fulfill your purpose. In other words, you know what you need to know. Through the process of activation, you build increasing levels of conscious comprehension. You begin gaining awareness, move to a sense of familiarity, and finally achieve the knowledge you desire.

Four levels of comprehension:
1) Awareness
2) Familiarity
3) Knowledge
4) Expertise

Activation after PhotoReading is quite different than trying to recall what you read in a regular manner. Activation techniques are designed to restimulate the new neural connections you created by PhotoReading, rather than trying to force recall through the critical/logical conscious mind.

You must be active and purposeful to gain conscious comprehension. During activation you find text relevant to your purpose. When you have no purpose for reading a document, generally little benefit can be gained from activation.

There are two types of activation: spontaneous and manual. *Spontaneous activation* occurs without conscious effort on your part. Perhaps you have had an "aha!" experience when you suddenly solved a problem that has preoccupied you for weeks, or saw the face of a friend in a crowd, or remembered the name of someone you met months ago.

Such activation is an automatic connection to past experiences, to neural patterns already existing in your brain. Stimuli in our environment and cues we may have not been looking for spontaneously trigger a flood of previous associations. Spontaneous activation feels similar to a flash of creative insight—sudden and unexpected.

Although PhotoReaders report many stories of spontaneous activation, they remain the cherry on top of the ice cream and are not the main entree of the PhotoReading whole mind system.

Manual activation, which is the focus of this chapter, means to activate by design. It uses the actual text as a catalyst for re-stimulating the brain, bringing the information you need into consciousness.

As you learn to activate, notice what you are feeling, doing, and thinking when experiences of awareness, familiarity, or knowledge occur. This careful observation will help you understand your own intuitive signals and further your activation skills. It is different for everyone, so uncover how it works for you.

There are five steps to activating:

1) Let it incubate

2) Review questions

3) Super read and dip

4) Create a mind map

5) Rapid read

1) Let it incubate

After PhotoReading and postviewing, you must dismiss the information from your conscious mind. That's right. Get away from it for a while. This act of creative procrastination helps you let it go while it incubates in your mind. To comprehend your reading you must give it over to your brain to work on. Wait at least ten to twenty minutes, or, if you can afford the luxury, overnight.

The concept of "initial effort followed by a period of incubation and rest" is well known to writers, artists, musicians, and scientists. It is not a period inactivity. Your brain never shuts off. It is on the job 24 hours each day. When you sleep, it creates dreams, generates solutions to gnawing problems you face at work, connects your current thoughts to a vast network of associated prior knowledge, and so on.

Let what you PhotoRead take its place in your brain, becoming integrated as part of the neural network. Activation will then cue up the associations your brain has constructed. You consciously connect and satisfy your purpose for reading.

One of our PhotoReading instructors told me a story of how easily the mind can use activation to accomplish reading goals. "A PhotoReading seminar student shared a poem with the word serendipity in it. That evening at my daughter's house, I wanted to look up the word. I walked into her den and went into PhotoFocus as I asked myself, 'What is here that will help me?' I hadn't even finished the question when my arm reached toward the bookshelf and grabbed a book. It happened to be the one my daughter had borrowed from me five months earlier, one I had only PhotoRead. I just let the book open to a page, and there on the bottom right corner of that page was Webster's definition of the word serendipity."

Obviously the expanded processing capability of the brain can work in wondrous ways. What more perfect way to explain what serendipity means than by offering a serendipitous experience? The point is, when you ask the mind properly, it works to give you what you want.

2) Review questions

After incubation review the questions formulated from your postview. The trigger words that you wrote down may have stimulated your curiosity in any one of several directions from the very general to the very specific. General questions could be, what is important to me in this book, article, or report? what are the main points? and what is in here that can help me? Specific questions could be, what do I need to know to perform well on the next test, to write my report, or contribute in the next meeting? Or, you may simply have come across a word or chapter heading that stimulated more questions. Questions probe your deeper, nonconscious memory storage system, opening a channel to the information and answers you desire. They stimulate a sense of curiosity. Reviewing your questions now causes the brain to find the best ways and means to achieve your purpose for the particular materials you are exploring.

As you ask questions of your mind, do not expect an immediate answer, although now and then you will get one. Expecting recall at this stage in activation can create frustration. When trying to recall information after PhotoReading, the conscious mind merely searches recent memory. Finding nothing, the conscious mind tends to shut off access to the vast nonconscious database of the brain. Reviewing your questions now helps you further decide which questions are most important for you right now. It initiates comprehension as it builds bridges to the expansive database of your brain where information resides after PhotoReading.

Reviewing your questions is the start of what activation is all about—actively putting your brain to work seeking the information that will satisfy your purpose. Holding a relevant question in mind, writing it on paper, or discussing it with another person initiates a search through the vast database that lies just below your everyday awareness. When you formulate questions, be sure to heighten the importance of the answers. The more you desire a response to your questions, the better.

Ask yourself questions in a state of relaxed alertness. Be genuinely curious and confident that answers can come. The results may pleasantly surprise you. The bridge between your conscious and preconscious database becomes sturdier when you consistently ask your mind to provide the answers you desire.

3) Super read and dip

Comprehension comes best in layers. The next layer of comprehension comes from super reading and dipping.

After reviewing your questions, go to the written materials and actively move through the text to uncover the answers you seek. What do you want to know from the text you are exploring? Where in the text can you go to find it? When super reading, the next step of activation, you quickly move through large blocks of information and locate the place where your answers reside.

First, you will turn to sections of the text that attract you in some way, based on your purpose for reading and the questions you want answered. "Visual cues" or clues in your materials give you a sense that certain sections are more important to you than other sections. These clues may include chapter titles or subheadings in the text that carry relevant information.

Then super read by rapidly moving your eyes down the center of each page looking for meaning in the section you have chosen. Your gaze must remain open. With a soft, open gaze, your eyes can move more smoothly down the text. At first, your visual field may be rather narrow. As you continue experimenting with noticing more, your visual field opens up so that you are able to see more words in the center of the column or page.

Try this: as you super read these words, notice whatever your peripheral vision picks up at the sides of you. You might lose the flow of the text temporarily, but do not let that distract you from the experiment. The moment you open your visual awareness, your gaze for the text in front of you becomes softer, less hard-focused. This permits you to relax and notice whatever catches your attention, whatever sentences or paragraphs attract you as being more important.

This is where you "dip" into the text, reading a sentence or two until you have received what you want from the passage. Then resume super reading.

 How do you know where to dip? Follow your hunches. Your brain has been exposed to the entire text by the PhotoReading technique, so let your internal signals at the periphery of your awareness be your guide. Do not worry about justifying your decision every time you decide to touch down for dipping; those signals are prelogical and preverbal. Monitored at the periphery of your conscious awareness, the signals come from connections made in the nonconscious database of your brain. Notice and heed them. Follow these hunches and discover where they lead you.

 In the PhotoReading seminar we often explain super reading with a visualization that is straight from those sacred bastions of American literature—comic books. Imagine that you are Superman coming to Earth for the first time.

From an aerial distance of one hundred thousand miles, you see Earth as a swirling blue ball. You set a flight path straight toward the planet. From ten thousand miles away, you can start to make out the outlines of continents. You also notice how much of the planet is covered by water. Zooming in closer, you notice the variegated land surfaces: deserts, rain forests, prairies, and mountains.

Suddenly, you are attracted to a lush, green island with a sandy beach surrounded by magnificent blue water. You touch down, spend a short time exploring the terrain, and take a quick dip in the water. Satisfied, you take to the skies again, searching for another place to land.

 This is a perfect metaphor for super reading and dipping. Super reading allows you to soar over the whole printed landscape. Dipping allows you to touch down on the parts of text that directly serve your purpose.

You can use the same technique when locating anything, by the way—not just places to dip into text. You can draw upon the vast knowledge within you in many situations.

My wife Libby went to a room at an estate sale in which old books were being sold. As she walked in, surrounded by floor-to-ceiling shelves full of books, she entered PhotoFocus. She asked herself "Is there an old or rare book in here that Paul would want?" Her eyes instantaneously flashed over to one book, which she walked across the room to pick up. It was the perfect book for me. Although her mind told her there were no others, she spent the next twenty minutes looking at every title, only to discover her mind was right—there were no others.

When super reading and dipping, follow your intuitive signals about where to look. Sometimes it is as simple as noticing where your eyes are pointing and choosing that direction. Sometimes you will find your hand just opens the book to the exact page. Pay attention. Notice whatever signals your mind offers.

Super reading and dipping, like all steps in the whole mind system, are strategies that keep you active, questioning, and alive to your purpose. You end up with enough information to make crucial decisions: where is the sentence or paragraph that sums up the essential point of this document? How much of this text is relevant to your purpose? Do you want to continue reading this or go to another source?

While dipping, you might experience a common problem. Your tendency, because of years of schooling and maybe even more years of reading, is to think you should dip into everything. If this happens, you are reading unnecessary details that do not serve your purpose. For example, you dip to read an illustration the author is making about an important point. That works. The next several paragraphs give additional, but redundant, illustrations. If you dip into those, you may just be wasting your time. If you waste too much time, you bog down in details and possibly veer off course into more irrelevant material.

That is when the old reading paradigm is often rearing its head. Your conscious mind may be on a guilt trip. For some of us it is as if our second or third grade teacher is reprimanding us by saying, "Stop! You missed a word. Go back over that more carefully. You are not really reading that. Now do it right!"

When you get these kinds of signals, thank that part of you for its concern. Let go of the worry that you are missing things as you super read. Your grade school-trained conscious mind wants you to read, comprehend, remember, and critique everything as you go. But, reading experts for over fifty years have said that is the worst way to read. Keep in mind that comprehension comes in layers. Each time you super read and dip, you peel back another layer of "not-knowing" to reveal what you need at the core of your text.

Trust your intuition and dip when you feel strongly moved to do so. If you dip into information you do not need, remember the purpose for your reading. Tell yourself to look for the spot where that information is contained and dip there. With a firm purpose your brain is free to use its natural ability to bring you to the information you need.

As reading authority Frank Smith points out in *Reading Without Nonsense*, making the effort to memorize the content as we read actually interferes with comprehension. As we worry about forgetting details, we create anxiety that blocks comprehension.

When in doubt, remember the vital statistic given by Russell Stauffer in his book *Teaching Reading as a Thinking Process*. He claims that only 4 to 11 percent of the text carries the essential meaning. In fact, a common way to test the readability of a text for a particular audience is to cross out four out of every five words. Then ask members of the intended audience to see if they can still sum up in a general way what the passage is about. If the text is written at an appropriate reading level, most audience members will be able to do this.

Tip) The best way to dip

When you stop to dip, limit your dipping to a paragraph or two at a time for articles and a page or two for books. Going back to our comic book analogy, as Superman you can savor the scenery and mingle with the locals later. Right now your overriding purpose is to keep exploring the planet, not to settle on the island and live out the rest of your days.

Read
Bullets

Dipping closely resembles regular reading, with a few important distinctions. Think of it as reading with a light, easy, and fluid movement. Dr. J. Michael Bennett, Professor Emeritus from the University of Minnesota calls it "rhythmic perusal." In his *Four Powers for Greatness Personal Learning Course,* published by Learning Strategies Corporation, he describes the process:

• Lock into your mind your purpose and the title or subtitle of the materials you are reading.

• Relax your face and eyes, and lightly focus in a way that allows you to move your gaze across the upper half of each sentence.

• Move across each line in a single smooth movement.

• Look for meaning units such as phrases.

• Read for thoughts, feelings, and ideas—not words.

In the scheme of the PhotoReading whole mind system, each time you super read and dip, you increase your familiarity with the text and add another layer of comprehension. You enter an intensive conversation with the author by posing questions and discovering the answers as you super read and dip. This is one of the most playful steps in the PhotoReading system.

As a PhotoReader, you are on a crusade for ideas that can help solve problems and raise the quality of your life. This is a dramatic quest worthy of any super hero.

When you make super reading and dipping part of your life, you may find ways to apply it beyond the written page. A jeweler who attends trade shows annually to purchase inventory decided to use the PhotoReading whole mind system to accomplish his goal at the trade show.

He stood at one end of the auditorium to get a panoramic view of the exhibits. He "PhotoRead" the entire place by walking quickly down each aisle in a PhotoFocus state. He called to mind the kind of stones he was looking for to fill his store's inventory and began "super reading" as he walked down one aisle at a time. Whenever he got a clear intuitive signal to go to a certain booth, he obeyed it and "dipped" in there.

Following this method, he managed to find all he needed in two hours. In previous years, his old method of methodically searching aisles usually took five days to accomplish the same end result.

As you integrate the PhotoReading whole mind system into your life, you will automatically do as the jeweler did. In this way, PhotoReading becomes an all-purpose tool. It is more than a technique for gathering information from books.

Tip) *Search for the train of thought*

When you super read and dip, go into the places where the value is greatest. Your brain is well trained by the time you are in ninth grade to know where to go in a text. It is skilled at searching for cues that lead to meaning.

For example, your brain knows that more visual cues occur in the upper half of our alphabet than in the lower half. Take a look at the following sentences:

Can you see what I mean about visual cues?

Do you find this easier or more difficult?

See? It is easier to make sense of the words when you see the upper half. Similarly, more cues for meaning show up in the topic sentence of a paragraph, than in the rest of the paragraph. And, in a five-paragraph theme, more cues appear in the first and last paragraphs.

When activating an article or book, look for the cues that will give you the most meaning. Look at the structure of the written piece and determine the author's scheme for writing. Then super read and dip to follow the author's scheme.

Here is what I mean. Perhaps you know that the author first describes a problem, and then later in the text explains how to solve the problem. Let us say you want the author's steps for solving the problem. Because you understand the author's scheme for writing, you can bypass what you do not need and move quickly to the place for dipping and achieving your goal.

We call this "following the author's train of thought." In the PhotoReading seminar I use an illustration to represent this:

- Problems identified by the author drive the train.

- Arguments about the problems are the main cargo in the flow of information. This cargo is built upon certain propositions the author is trying to sell you.

- Solutions emerge to suggest a remedy for the problems.

The train of thought is one scheme used by authors to present information. Discover other structures within articles or books. These structures for presenting information show you where to super read and dip to quickly get the information you need.

Finally, although the super reading and dipping strategies may sound like conventional speed reading, they are not. Super reading and dipping take place after you PhotoRead—after exposing the entire text to your brain and connecting into it with your nonconscious memory storage system. So super reading and dipping help you consciously connect to the vast database already within and recognize what you know to be important. Speed reading is merely a method to consciously read faster.

In addition, the goal is not to memorize the material or make it all available to the conscious mind. Instead, super reading and dipping help you sense structure, retrieve essential information, categorize the material in a meaningful way, and build a mental summary. As a result, your comprehension and long-term retention of the material increases.

Tip) Skittering as an alternative to dipping

PhotoReaders who have strong preference for analytical thinking find that an alternative to super reading and dipping works well. "Skittering," a technique developed by Dr. J. Michael Bennett, gives analytical minds a feeling of greater security while still allowing for rapid movement through text. Bennett presents skittering in the *Four Powers for Greatness Personal Learning Course* as a technique that exceeds the performance of speed reading techniques. Skittering also offers a valuable alternative to dipping.

Skittering achieves very fast and surprisingly accurate understanding of lengthy material that is informative or instructional in nature. Skittering can be used to cover an entire text or section of a book as well as between areas that you super read. In other words, you could "super read and dip," "super read and skitter," or just "skitter" a book, journal, report, and various electronic documents. As you experiment with these techniques, you will discover what works best for you and the material you are reading.

The term skittering describes a wild, dancing-about movement like that of a water bug on the surface of a pond. It involves rapid, erratic movement of your eyes through a paragraph to give your brain an opportunity to look at all of the words that support the paragraph's main premise. Consistent with the idea that only 4 to 11 percent of a text carries meaning, skittering over all the words lets your brain capture the important ones and feel secure in passing over the rest of them.

Here are the steps to use skittering as an activation technique. The word "read" means rhythmic perusal—the style of reading used earlier to describe dipping.

• Read the first sentence (also known as the topic sentence) of the paragraph you are going to skitter.

Read
Bullets

• Move your eyes in a rapid pattern over all the words in the paragraph, except those in the first and last sentence. Notice words that seem to support the premise in the first sentence. The movement of your eyes can follow a zigzag from top to bottom or bottom to top. It can follow circular pattern clockwise or counterclockwise and move from the center out or from the edges into the center. There is no set pattern, but you will discover a preference for one of them. Play with them all to find what works best for you. This movement gives your brain a chance to spot ideas that augment or add to the main concept in a paragraph.

• If the meaning of the paragraph remains unclear, read the last sentence. Continue this process through each succeeding paragraph until you near the end of the reading selection.

4) Create a mind map

While looking through a box of my old graduate school materials, I discovered a wonderful contrast between two types of class notes. One type of notes was the traditional linear outline of everything the professor said—an endless series of unintelligible scratching and unfinished sentences. I remembered trying to decipher those notes while reviewing for tests–what a horrid chore.

The second type of notes was an alternative, highly visual set of colorful diagrams called "mind maps." They reminded me how fun it was to create and review class information. Looking them over brought back a flood of vivid details. Mind mapping, as it is called, had transformed my classroom experience forever.

Mind mapping is fast and highly efficient. It promotes long-term retention and helps synthesize information after super reading and dipping.

The mind map on the next page sums up the five steps of the PhotoReading whole mind system.

Mind mapping uses keyword notes. This process eliminates ninety percent of the unnecessary note-making, improving your effective writing/note-making speed by as much as ten times. In addition to this advantage, your recall will also be greatly improved, because you will not have to waste time sifting through all the unnecessary words.

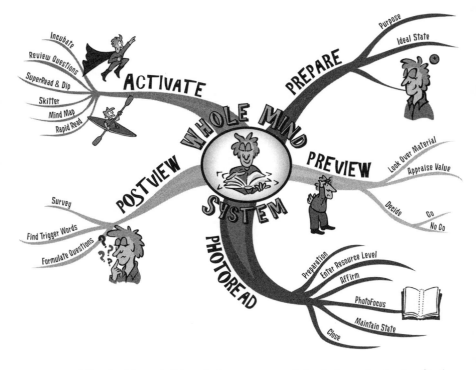

After looking at this mind map, you might deduce the basic guidelines for the technique:

- Put the core concept in the center of the page.

- Write supporting concepts on connecting lines radiating from the center.

Read Bullets

- Use key terms only—often they will be trigger words identified in your postview. Express each concept in three words or less.

- Include visual elements—cartoons, images, symbols, icons— wherever they seem appropriate.

- Add color. In the above mind map, for example, all the words pertaining to Step 1 could be written in one color, all those for Step 2 in a second color, and so on.

Two of the best books on mind mapping explain this technique in more detail. They are *The Mind Map Book* by Tony Buzan and *Mind Mapping* by Joyce Wycoff.

When mind mapping, consider using sheets of paper that are larger than standard paper. If you do stick to standard-sized paper, at least turn the paper sideways so that you are writing on a horizontal frame. Most people find this gives them more room to record ideas.

Mind maps are highly individual. Your mind maps will look different from anyone else's, even if you are making notes on the same material. That is okay. Ideally, your mind map reflects your experience. The images and associations that promote your long-term memory are unique to you.

Even if it feels awkward at first, play with mind mapping as an activation exercise. Because mind mapping uses visual memory and spatial intelligence, it accesses the most powerful memory centers of the brain. Moreover, mind mapping mirrors the way the mind works—linking ideas through branches of association rather than linear logic. Perhaps that is why mind maps begin to feel so natural so soon.

Mind mapping can serve you in two ways. First, it can provide another layer of comprehension immediately—it can even stimulate a recall of more information. Second, it can be a trigger for rapid recall of information at a later time. If you choose to mind map a book, consider keeping the mind map in the book itself. When you revisit the mind map in the future, the content of the book will flood back with more richness than simply looking at the table of contents or traditional notes.

Mind mapping is optional. When you are learning PhotoReading, use it on all books that you choose to activate until you discover the ways it serves you best.

Tip) Gain a new experience of memory

The paradigm shift we advocate for reading also applies to memory. It is the combination of activation techniques that improves your overall memory dramatically and immediately. To understand how this happens we need to reconsider the role of memory.

I have been fascinated by the work of Gerald Edelman, a Nobel prize-winning neurologist and author of *The Remembered Present* and *Bright Air, Brilliant Fire*. Edelman's ideas offer the most convincing explanation I have yet found for what may be happening when we activate material.

Edelman's theory claims that memories are not stored in a localized fashion in the brain but are reinvented each time we access them. What happens when we remember is that we create a mental context for an idea, re-enter important cues or bits of related information, and follow neural "tracks" that have been laid by previous experience. When enough cues are entered and the correct neural pathways are stimulated, the ideas and images we want to "remember" are not recalled from storage but are recreated right on the spot.

Applying this view to PhotoReading and activating, we begin to understand what might be happening to produce such remarkable results. When we PhotoRead, the brain processes written materials more physiologically than cognitively. That physical exposure to the brain opens neural networks inside the brain that can lead to later mental connections.

The result is increased speed, familiarity, and ease of comprehension. You will have the ability to connect with the most important information almost instantly, rather than trying to figure it out as you read. You do not have to waste time investing hours in a book to get the knowledge you want.

This is much like laying a set of railroad tracks for a train to travel on later. PhotoReading lays in the tracks. When we activate the material, we re-enter the original information through super reading and dipping or skittering, and the conscious mind follows the tracks to the destination of full comprehension.

I admit I cannot do justice to Edelman's theory of memory in a few short paragraphs. It is far more important for you to experience this process rather than have me try to explain it. The activation processes of incubation, reviewing questions, super reading and dipping, skittering, and mind mapping are all gateways to that experience.

5) Rapid Read

During the PhotoReading seminar I ask participants a question after we have prepared, previewed, PhotoRead, postviewed, super read and dipped in a book: "How many of you would still like to get more from this book?" Usually, 40 percent of them will raise their hands. Then I ask, "What specifically would you like to get from the book?"

To this question, several reply precisely. They know exactly which parts of the book they may want to study in more detail. For them, the next step is additional super reading and dipping to complete their goal.

Sometimes, however, you get to a chapter that is really important to you or that is so technical that you need a more detailed conversation with the author. This is where the final part of activation, rapid reading, can best be utilized. There are also authors who write in such a way that their words deserve to be savored.

The choice to rapid read is made when you know you want more from the text, and the laser-like precision of super reading and dipping will not bring you there. It also serves you best for pleasure or leisure reading when you desire to immerse yourself in the feelings an author evokes in you.

Rapid reading is similar to speed reading with two significant differences. First, rapid reading is the final decision of the PhotoReading whole mind system. Second, the speed of rapid reading is highly flexible.

To rapid read, move swiftly through the text, taking as much time as you need. Go from start to finish of the section, chapter, or book. Depending on the complexity and importance of a particular passage, vary your speed.

Read Bullets

You will rapid read faster when:

• You have already read that paragraph or page during one of the other steps. Zip past it.

• You recognize that the information is simplistic, redundant, understood, or unnecessary. Zip past it.

• You quickly see that the section you are reading is unimportant to your purpose so you can flash past at PhotoReading speeds keeping your intuition open to stop you if it tells you to check something out.

You will read slower when:

• The text contains unfamiliar information.

• You sense complex information that needs more careful consideration.

• You recognize an extremely important passage you want to explore in more detail.

The end result is that you move at varying speeds through the text: sometimes faster, sometimes slower depending upon importance, complexity, and your prior knowledge of the information.

An essential point in rapid reading is that you keep moving. Never pause to struggle with information you might not understand. It is common to stop when you do not fully understand what you are reading. That is part of the old paradigm. Instead, just keep reading. Comprehension comes best in layers.

When you stop and try to wrestle with what you do not know, you can get sidetracked and never finish. When you keep going, soon you will come to information you do understand—discovering clues in the text that answer the questions you were stuck on previously. By staying in a relaxed, alert state with rapid reading, you keep extracting the information you want—information that relates directly to your purpose.

Tip) Use rapid reading when reading for pleasure

When you want to read for pleasure or to simply pass time, you will find great value in first PhotoReading the book and then rapid reading it. This process works for both fiction as well as nonfiction. You will find the writing richer, fuller, and more enjoyable, because a part of you has already processed the material, making connections on a deeper level that you simply cannot make when you merely read a book. As an early PhotoReading student said, "I have rediscovered the joy of reading."

> Practicing rhythmic perusal with your rapid reading helps improve the speed and therefore the comprehension of the material you are enjoying.

Tip) Rapid read or super read?

A common question is: how does rapid reading differ from super reading? At first glance, the two steps might seem similar. Rapid reading, however, proceeds straight through the text from beginning to end of an important chapter or the entire book. Super reading seeks out sections of the text you are attracted to and zips lightly down the center of the page locating answers to questions you have.

Rapid reading might involve slowing down to a more conventional reading speed; you might do this to comprehend a technical drawing or mathematical formula, or to savor a line of poetry. In contrast, super reading means maintaining a brisk speed and dipping into the text when a possible answer is located; there is no requirement to move through the pages in order.

Super reading has been compared to the actions of a Superman scanning the Earth from outer space and deciding to touch down on certain continents. We need another analogy for rapid reading— perhaps that of taking a river kayak trip. Sometimes you career over white water rapids, then paddle leisurely on placid waters. Then you might be back to rapids again. The point is that we stay active and alert, and our speed varies depending on the material being covered.

Rapid reading is not always necessary. At times, previewing, PhotoReading, postviewing, and the first techniques of activating may be all you need to attain your desired reading outcome. Many business people never need to use the technique of rapid reading. When reading business-related information, such as reports and manuals, they achieve their purpose using the other techniques of activation.

Students studying a textbook and people reading for pleasure will use rapid reading quite often, because it gives the conscious mind more to explore.

PhotoReaders who enjoy reading novels will preview, PhotoRead, then move directly into rapid reading, bypassing the other activation techniques altogether. Play with the wonderful options the PhotoReading whole mind system provides you. You will find the best path to achieve your purpose for reading.

Tip) Demonstrate how the system works for you

The rapid reading technique is reassuring, because it builds full conscious comprehension of the materials you are studying. Like the other manual activation techniques, rapid reading works mostly with the conscious mind.

As you achieve your reading goals using the PhotoReading whole mind system, you might wonder which step is having the greatest impact upon your success. It will be easy to assume that the techniques involving the conscious mind are the biggest contributors, because you gain conscious comprehension when you use them. It may be difficult to think the nonconscious step of PhotoReading really did anything at all.

The system works because it is a *whole mind* system. Both the conscious mind and the nonconscious mind participate. By all means, enjoy the benefits you receive consciously. At the same time, keep noticing other positive effects in your life that are assigned to the domain of the nonconscious mind.

The most stunning demonstrations of the PhotoReading step often come as spontaneous activation. Stories of spontaneous activation from PhotoReading graduates are wonderful encouragement to all beginning PhotoReaders. They all have similar characteristics.

The reports sound like this: "I was in the situation in which I needed or wanted some information, and it showed up. I was not even trying at the time to remember it. It just happened. The information just appeared, just popped into mind, not because I was trying to recall it, but almost on a whim."

The "aha!" experience of spontaneous activation is a convincing demonstration. It has been proof for many people that the PhotoReading step of the system is actually working for them. The paradox is, how do you plan to have a spontaneous experience? You cannot—because it must be spontaneous.

Do not sit around waiting for spontaneous activation experiences. There are other ways to test the system. In my original studies of PhotoReading I had compelling evidence that PhotoReading was working. Some evidence came from spontaneous activation, but mostly it came from manual activation techniques.

For the first year of my graduate studies, I did not have the PhotoReading whole mind system. In the remaining eighteen months, I used PhotoReading for everything. The contrast was enormous. I kept on top of every subject, completing reading assignments and research reports with ease. The pressures of keeping up with my studies vanished.

Since those early days of PhotoReading, I have consistently seen that students in school have the best ongoing demonstrations that PhotoReading works. Why? Because they are using and testing the system all the time, both objectively and subjectively.

If you are not in school, you need to set up your own measures. Create a convincing experience of PhotoReading. Here are some ways you might test it for yourself:

Read Bullets

• For one week, PhotoRead everything and activate anything that you need to comprehend. The next week, go back to regular reading without PhotoReading. Decide which week was most productive.

• When you see a book at a friend's house that he has recently read, ask if it was worth reading and how long it took to read. Borrow the book and spend one-tenth the time with the book (or one-third the time if you are less daring), using the five steps of the PhotoReading whole mind system. Then, get together with your friend and discuss the book, without mentioning that this is your own private test. Afterward, let your friend decide if you understood the book.

• Find a quiet time to notice the way your brain responds to PhotoReading. Select a novel with high emotional content such as a lusty romance novel or a suspense thriller, because high emotions can stimulate visceral responses. Then, go in a room with few distractions. Light only the book so you can see little else, keep the room quiet, wear comfortable clothing, and maintain a comfortable room temperature. The idea is to make it as easy as possible to notice whatever comes up from the nonconscious memory stores. Take a few moments to study the images and feelings within you. Then PhotoRead, noticing any thoughts (pictures, sounds, feelings, etc.) that come into awareness. If a picture or strong feeling pops into your mind, turn back a few pages and read the text. Compare how your inner experience matches the content of the book. You may have thoughts of a skiing vacation and then discover that the characters in the book were skiing!

After PhotoReading and using your closing affirmations, look around in your inner quiet scene again. Notice any changes in the images, sounds, or feelings within you. Take two minutes to draw pictures that you see in mind or to represent any emotions you feel. You can then go back through the book to see how your experience matches the content of the book. Or, better yet, tell someone who knows the book what you experienced and then let them tell you about the story.

• Before a business meeting, preview and PhotoRead five books related to the topic you will discuss at the meeting. Afterward, consider how your performance may have differed from your usual performance at such meetings.

 All of those tests are easy and low-risk. They allow you to explore uses of the PhotoReading whole mind system. Play with them and have compelling demonstrations of your own.

You do not have to stop here. There are many ways to extend the steps introduced so far. Use the suggestions in the remaining chapters to discover more applications for PhotoReading. Make it a skill you use daily for all your reading needs.

Tip) Take the five-day test

When you want a strong way to convince yourself that your brain can PhotoRead successfully, here is a revealing test you should consider. It reliably demonstrates the power of PhotoReading and doubles as a five-day plan for improving activation. Investing thirty minutes or less per day, the plan helps condition you to get what you want and need from books you PhotoRead. Commit to following:

Day 1 - Select a book you are interested in reading. Prepare and PhotoRead the book.

Day 2 - Prepare, preview for no more than one minute, and PhotoRead the book. Postview for 10 to 15 minutes, including writing trigger words and formulating questions you are eager to answer.

Day 3 - Prepare and PhotoRead. Then super read and dip so that you get through the entire book in the thirty minutes. Do not worry about comprehension. At the end, review your trigger words to get a feeling for how much recognition may be coming together for you.

Day 4 - Prepare and PhotoRead. Spend the rest of the thirty minutes super reading and dipping or skittering the entire book, at a pace that will get you through the book by the end of the session. Again, look at your trigger words, and formulate additional questions.

Day 5 - Prepare and PhotoRead. Look at the Table of Contents and go to the sections that you feel you need more information. Super read and dip or skitter to answer specific questions. Rapid read if you do not have specific questions but want more information. Save ten minutes at the end to mind map the book. Keep it simple, limiting the amount of detail. The goal is not to mind map the entire contents of the book, but to mind map the book as it relates to your purpose for choosing the book in the first place.

At this point you have spent two hours plus a bit. Most people will see the book coming together for them. Many feel they have enough information and that they know the book. The goal is not to know the book 100 percent—that doesn't even happen with regular reading. You may want to spend two more "Day 4s," but it is likely you will say that you know everything in the book you need. You may find it fun to review your mind map after a few days to recognize your grasp of the material. Overall, you should finish with the book in about one-third the time it would take to read the book in the traditional manner.

Tip) Spontaneous activation

While this chapter focuses on the most reliable forms of activation, I would like to give you the secret of PhotoReaders who have multiple experiences with spontaneous activation. Here it is: PhotoRead three to five, even five to ten, books a day for two or three months. With that many PhotoReading sessions you are bound to experience spontaneous activation. Once you experience it, keep PhotoReading day after day. Remember, success breeds success. Soon you will have another experience of spontaneous activation as your brain works to create more success for you.

With that many PhotoReading sessions the entire PhotoReading system will become second nature for you. And if you also fully activate a book or two each week, you'll find your confidence with manual activation skyrocketing!

In review of the ideas of this chapter, you learned:

• There are two types of activation: spontaneous and manual. This chapter is concerned with manual activation.

• Clear purpose and strong questions are essential for activation.

• After PhotoReading and postviewing it is best to wait at least twenty minutes, but ideally 24 hours, before activating.

• Super reading and dipping involve moving quickly over sections of text that attract you, then reading selected passages that answer your questions. It goes for the essence.

• An understanding of the author's scheme or structure will help guide your super reading and dipping.

• Skittering is an activation technique that is designed to give you greater detail. You rhythmically peruse the first line of each paragraph. Next, you allow your eyes to randomly move through the remainder of the paragraph, picking up words and phrases that support the first sentence. Skittering allows you to acquire higher levels of comprehension.

• Mind mapping is a highly visual and spatial way to take notes. It helps activate materials because it uses the whole mind.

Activation stimulates the brain, giving cues to the associations your brain has constructed. As a result, you consciously meet your needs and satisfy your purpose for reading.

Part Three:

Develop and Integrate Your Skills

8

Make the PhotoReading Whole Mind System Part of Your Daily Life

Read
Bullets

Now that you have been exposed to the steps of the system, you can certainly apply them to this book, if you have not done so already. Here are my suggestions on how to proceed.

• Using this book, which you know can support you in your current life goals, establish a clear purpose for reading and enter the ideal state of mind.

• Preview the book for one minute going over the table of contents.

• PhotoRead the book by following the steps of the procedure in Chapter 5. You can PhotoRead this book in fewer than three minutes by flipping a page every two seconds. When finished, give yourself the closing affirmations and relax for a few moments.

• Ideally, get up and take a short break. Then come back to postview.

• Play with the book to discover more of the structure, write down some trigger words and then formulate your questions. Activate by super reading and dipping, or skittering. Concentrate on activating the remaining chapters of this book. Take no more than twenty or thirty minutes for this.

• Review and summarize all you gathered during your first activation session with a one-page mind map of the entire book.

• Take a minute to affirm your ability to apply these advanced reading strategies in your daily life. As you do so, you are taking action that could change the way you read forever.

• Finish by rapid reading the last section of this book. This is your chance to discover how much faster your reading has become by using the tremendously flexible skills you have learned.

Five instant time management strategies

Organizing your time and reading materials can enhance your use of the PhotoReading whole mind system. Use these strategies and discover the benefits.

1) Prioritize your reading. Sort your printed materials into three levels of priority: "A" for matters that are urgent, "B" for items that are important but not urgent, and "C" for items that can be thrown away. Begin using the PhotoReading whole mind system with the "A" priority items.

2) Handle papers only once. Decide how you will respond to each piece of paper the first time you read it. Jot your decision right on letters and memos.

3) Always carry reading materials with you. Use waiting time for reading. You will be surprised how much you can accomplish in the five or ten minutes between appointments using the whole mind system.

4) Preview everything that is important. If you do nothing else with it, at least preview a document for thirty seconds before filing it.

5) Use the PhotoReading whole mind system at every opportunity. PhotoRead everything you can get your hands on. When the quarterly trade journal arrives or the weekly news magazine is delivered, PhotoRead them. Just take a moment to drop into state and flip the pages before your PhotoFocused eyes. Even if you do not activate, the exposure can serve you in the future.

Use the PhotoReading whole mind system all of the time

PhotoReading can accommodate all printed material. This includes letters, email, memos, web pages, newspapers, trade journals, magazines, novels, textbooks, technical manuals—any documents that you encounter in daily life. As you work with these materials, feel free to adapt the strategies of the system and you will significantly reduce the time you spend on routine reading.

Read
Bullets

• Daily news—Investing a few minutes a day will build a powerful momentum that lets you blast through newspapers at tremendous rates. In many metropolitan newspapers, journalists are required to put 90 percent of the relevant information in the title, subtitle, and first paragraphs of their articles. You can leverage this fact to keep on top of the news.

Start by PhotoReading the entire newspaper. Try standing up and setting the paper on a table in front of you so that you can PhotoFocus at the center of the open paper. Then notice any headlines that catch your attention, based on your purposes or needs. Select three to five articles that carry the highest value and preview each for thirty seconds. If you desire more information, super read and dip to capture the core concept. In most cases, today's news was previewed yesterday, and will conclude tomorrow. Use the PhotoReading whole mind system to spot relevant information, quickly grab it, and move on. At the end of the day, scan the newspaper for anything else you might want to read in more detail. You will discover a growing confidence that you have acquired what you need.

• Magazines—Be playful. Consider browsing from back to front if you like. Go to the articles that contain information you desire. PhotoRead then postview each of those articles. Limit your postviewing to no more than three minutes for the longer articles. Super read and dip or skitter to get the core concepts you want. You can activate most ten-page articles in five minutes. You can finish shorter articles much more quickly. After covering all you need, determine if you want anything more.

• Journals—These should be read with a cross between magazine strategies and textbook strategies. My favorite technique involves a brief preview of the table of contents. PhotoRead the entire journal and follow it with a few minutes of postviewing to determine which articles deserve more time. Rank the articles by importance and begin activation with the most important one. If the publication provides an abstract or summary at the beginning of an article, rapid read that and then briefly preview the article. Finish your activation with a quick super read and dip, or you may want to skitter it to get what you need. Mind mapping can serve you if you want to capture and retain written notes for future use.

• Novels—Some readers enjoy reading a book as much or more than going to the movies. I found out that when my whole mind is engaged, reading a novel is more exciting than a movie. I prepare as usual by fixing my tangerine point and entering the ideal state of mind. Next, I preview the story, looking for the names of significant persons, places, and things. Then I PhotoRead the book, which, of course, does not spoil the ending. Finally, I follow PhotoReading with rapid reading. Super reading and dipping serve little or no purpose for enjoyment of a story.

• Textbooks or technical manuals—A strategy of previewing followed by PhotoReading is the ideal start. Determine the chapters or major sections you want to activate first. Choose your activation steps according to how much of the content you want to recall at a conscious level. I usually start with summary questions at the end of a chapter to formulate my own questions. With a purpose clearly in mind and questions well formulated, you can use super reading and dipping or skittering to gather the information you need. Here you might choose to eliminate the rapid reading step unless there is a particular area you need to understand at a deeper level. If you are a student needing to study for school or a professional returning to classes for professional development and continuing education, read the section coming up titled "Study with your whole mind."

Read
Bullets

Email, web pages, and electronic files

One executive bemoaned the deluge of information coming to her each day. "If I am away from my office for a day or two, I return to an email in-box with over one hundred emails!" Another executive using the PhotoReading whole mind system boasted that in less than ten seconds per page he could digest email text and enter meetings fully prepared. "Now I need a class on PhotoTyping!"

Studies have shown that people read from computer screens at rates 25 percent slower than when reading printed materials. Speed of transmission across the Internet used to be the biggest problem in information transfer. Now it appears that getting the information from the screen and into the mind for processing has become the biggest challenge. Related problems of low screen resolution, poor writing quality, and inadequate organization of material will not slow down the PhotoReader. The PhotoReading whole mind system trains the brain to quickly locate units of meaning and respond with purpose, without wasting time and energy focusing on each word or sentence in an electronic text.

Short electronic files, web pages, and email are best handled with previewing followed by rapid reading. Longer pieces are best handled using the full system. The speed at which electronic pages can flash on the screen adds a thrilling dimension to PhotoReading. It is not unusual for someone to PhotoRead at speeds from 100,000 to 1,000,000 words a minute.

Tens of thousands of books are already available on the Internet for PhotoReading. You can PhotoRead many books in a web browser while others require downloading onto a computer to be viewed in a word processing program. A show produced by a British television company and presented on The Learning Channel showed the program's host Paul McKenna PhotoReading novels on the Internet. He and others PhotoRead at rates up to 1,000,000 words a minute, and they answered test questions at over 70 percent comprehension.

Read Bullets

When you want to read electronic files, you should make the same decisions to set your purpose, preview, PhotoRead, postview to create questions you want to answer, super read and dip, skitter, and rapid read as you would with regular books. However, the mechanics of those steps will change due to the high speeds possible using computers. Consider the following modifications.

• PhotoFocus—Because electronic files are usually not presented on two side-by-side pages, as is a book, you will not be able to see the blip page. Simply expand your peripheral vision so you can view all four corners of the screen; let your eyes soften. Less experienced PhotoReaders should follow the alternate PhotoFocus strategies presented in Chapter 5. A soft gaze at the center of the computer screen as text flashes seems the best strategy for the PhotoReading step.

• Page flipping—There are no pages to turn on the computer, so this becomes fast and easy. "Scrolling" through text tends to be more confusing to the brain than using the "page down" and "page up" functions on the keypad. Transferring large files into a word processing program and manipulating it with these functions makes for easy PhotoReading. Then, use the scrolling function to move through text for the other steps of the system.

Study with your whole mind

The PhotoReading whole mind system naturally creates a perfect strategy for moving through a semester of reading. Imagine previewing and PhotoReading every book for the entire semester on the first day of class. Throughout the night, in your dream state, the material is reviewed and organized according to your needs and purpose.

Before you begin your class, decide what you want as an initial purpose. Preview the Table of Contents of the entire text and PhotoRead it. If it is a difficult subject for you, you might want to PhotoRead the same text several times in the first few weeks with a different purpose each time.

When you receive a reading assignment for a textbook, preview and PhotoRead the chapters, plus PhotoRead one or two chapters on either side of them. For example, if you are assigned Chapters 3 and 4, preview those and PhotoRead Chapters 2 through 5. Use rhythmic perusal to read the chapter summary and study questions at the end of the assigned chapters. Then, super read and dip to find the answers to the questions.

When you attend class, you naturally and spontaneously activate the chapters. Create mind maps during the lecture for all your class notes. For instant review of the entire lecture, take your multiple mind maps and combine them into one. Determine if you need anything else from the reading assignment. When you need specific information, super read and dip to find it. To handle vague feelings of uncertainty, use skittering or rapid reading to cover anything else you want to study in the chapters. Mind map important points that you need to memorize, such as specific facts, formulas, theorems, and historical events.

Before writing reports, use syntopic reading described in Chapter 11. You can preview and PhotoRead dozens of books on the subject of your report. Then super read and dip in the most important texts to get the core concepts you need. Mind map your first draft and write your report from your mind map.

When studying for tests, look over your mind maps, PhotoRead your assignments to get yourself in the flow state, then use rapid reading to review chapters assigned for the test. The night before an exam, listen to the *Memory Supercharger* Paraliminal CD.

With these potent study skills, the ease and pleasure of learning will astound you. A PhotoReader, attending a college humanities class had nine books to study during the semester. With one book over six hundred pages long, she invested fewer than thirty minutes whole mind reading in order to write a paper that received an A grade. She received an A for the semester and claimed she had spent about two hours total using the system.

If you doubt the story, prove it to yourself. Experiment with the following procedure as you study. The idea here is to study in blocks of twenty to thirty minutes, which contain mental preparation and physical breaks. The effect is an increase in concentration, retention, and recall of all you study.

1) Gather all the reading materials you intend to use during the study session. Lay them out in front of you.

2) Take three to five minutes to state your purpose and enter the ideal state of mind. When stating your purpose consider your desired outcome for this study session. Enter the ideal state for learning and repeat affirmations. Phrase your affirmation in the present tense. For example:

• I am ready to absorb Chapters 5 and 6 of this physics text to prepare for class tomorrow and answer the questions at the end of the chapter.

• As I study for the next twenty minutes, I do so with full alertness and effortless concentration.

• When I am through studying, I feel refreshed, relaxed, and confident.

• When I call upon this information in the future, I relax and let go. The information flows freely through my mind. I easily retrieve the information I desire.

3) Begin your study in the flow state of relaxed alertness. Preview the material briefly, then for the remainder of the twenty minutes use whatever combination of PhotoReading, activating, or rapid reading suits your purpose. Go for zero distractions.

4) Take a five-minute break. This is essential. Move completely away from your study area, both physically and mentally. Even if you are on a roll and feel as though you could study for hours, take the break! You affirmed a specific time commitment of twenty minutes. Keep your commitment, because it not only builds self trust, the break also helps your brain absorb, retain, and recall information you study.

5) Go back to Step 2 and repeat the cycle two more times. Then give yourself a 15-minute break before beginning another set of three study cycles.

Playing pleasant music softly in the background as you study may add to your relaxation. Studies have found that classical and New Age music can help make a greater impact on the brain while learning. The Paraliminal CD *Personal Genius* is extremely valuable prior to studying, because it boosts confidence and trains your body/mind to enter the ideal learning state. The *Memory Supercharger* Paraliminal CD helps after studying to solidify learning and before tests to aid in fluent recall.

Take tests with your whole mind

When taking tests on materials you have studied using the whole mind system, follow these tips:

- **Get into the ideal state of relaxed alertness.**
- **PhotoRead all the questions.** Then read the first question.
- **Answer all the questions that come easily first.** Stay focused on the present moment. Let go of the previous question, as well as any anticipation of the next question.
- **If an answer does not come to you after reading a question, let it go and move to the next question.** The request for an answer to the earlier question has already been given to your mind. When you have answered all the questions that come easily, go back and reread those you passed up. The second reading reinforces the request and helps the appropriate answers appear in your conscious mind.
- **Discover how your deeper mind signals you** that it has a correct or appropriate answer to a test question. Rather than overanalyzing the test question, study the response your brain offers as you notice your intuitive signals. For example, imagine a traffic light that will give you direction. Green means go. Yellow means maybe you know the answer, but you should proceed cautiously. Red means stop; do not answer this one.
- **Release any need you may have to perform well.** The results of any single test fade in importance over time. More often than not, force only leads to frustration. Get what you need by letting go of your need to have it.
- **When taking tests, pause many times to relax and breathe deeply.**
- **The night before your exam, listen to audio CDs** such as *Memory Supercharger* and *Personal Genius* that promote relaxation, learning, and memory skills.

Integrate your skills

You are born with a brain equipped for PhotoReading. However, you are not born with all the skills of the PhotoReading whole mind system. The system—a cluster of learned skills—must be used in order to integrate them and make them second nature to you.

PhotoReading and the other steps in the system are learned just like any other skill, such as playing the piano or using a personal computer. If you want to turn a new skill into a habit, follow the strategy of learning specialists David W. Johnson from the University of Minnesota and Frank P. Johnson from the University of Maryland. You can apply their approach to learning the skills of the PhotoReading whole mind system:

• **Understand why the skills are important and how they will be of value to you.** To learn a skill, you must feel a need for it. Your determination means everything. Determine that you want these skills and the results they will produce.

• **Understand the outcome of using the skills and master their component behaviors.** Using the PhotoReading whole mind system helps you to get your reading done in the time you have available at the level of comprehension you need. This larger skill consists of five steps: preparing, previewing, PhotoReading, postviewing, and activating. Each step contains a sequence of component behaviors. Perform the behaviors according to the instructions several times until you know the sequence of steps to perform.

Often it helps to observe someone who has already mastered the skill perform it several times. Attending a live PhotoReading seminar or listening to the *PhotoReading Personal Learning Course* provides coaching as you examine and perform each component behavior in a step-by-step manner. Once you know which skills you want to perform, with mental rehearsal and skilled practice you can quickly acquire them. The Paraliminal CD titled *New Behavior Generator* helps remove barriers to learning and guides your mind to install the new skills in your ongoing behavior.

• **Find situations in which you can use the skills.** To master a skill, use it again and again. Use the skill for a short time each day in a variety of settings. The *Belief* or *PhotoReading Activator* Paraliminal CDs help you develop your capabilities as a PhotoReader and build the confidence for stretching beyond previous comfort zones.

• **Ask someone to watch and tell you how well you are performing.** Getting feedback is necessary for staying on course to your goal. In the PhotoReading seminar and personal learning course, we guide you through PhotoReading books, explore various forms of activation, and provide numerous assessments of your progress that give you direct feedback.

• **Be persistent.** Keep doing it! There is a rhythm to learning most skills: a period of slow learning followed by a period of fast improvement and then a period in which performance remains about the same. These plateaus are quite common in skill learning. If you encounter one, just keep using the skill and remind yourself that another period of rapid improvement is on the way. The *Automatic Pilot* Paraliminal CD facilitates the effective use of any skill. It helps you eliminate self-sabotage and accomplish goals with greater ease.

• **Load your learning toward success.** As you stretch your capacity, add refinements that you can easily master. For example, using a stopwatch, determine how long it takes to read the morning newspaper in your usual manner. Then do same level of reading in five minutes less time tomorrow. Accomplish this by refining your use of previewing, super reading and dipping, or skittering.

• **Ask friends to encourage you to use the skill.** When you take a PhotoReading seminar, you will have the opportunity to exchange support with other PhotoReaders. The best support network you will ever find for your use of PhotoReading is the people with whom you attend the seminar or who use the *PhotoReading Personal Learning Course*. Share the PhotoReading idea with supportive friends and have them cheer you on. The PhotoReading discussion forum at www.LearningStrategies.com/forum can also be very supportive for you.

• **Use the skills until they feel real.** The more you use a skill, the more natural it becomes. While learning a skill, you may feel self-conscious and awkward. It may seem as though you are simply going through the motions. Do not let this normal awkwardness stop you from mastering the skill. People do not learn to type by typing only when it feels natural. It is through using the techniques and working through the initial discomfort that skills are learned.

In summary, it is up to you to apply the techniques presented in this book and apply them in ways that achieve your purposes. If you want to master whole mind reading, then follow these three suggestions: use it, use it, and use it.

Avoid creating an artificial "practice time." This can become drudgery. You have reading you want and need to do. Use the system! You may even consider enrolling in a PhotoReading seminar or listening to the *PhotoReading Personal Learning Course*. Meanwhile, dig into those piles of books lying around the house.

Choose how you will use the PhotoReading whole mind system

As you finish this chapter, think of a specific reading task that you often face, such as reading reports and trade journals, studying textbooks, or cruising the Internet. Use the PhotoReading whole mind reading system in ways that will accomplish your goal.

Imagine how and when you will use the techniques. For example, you might see yourself previewing the morning paper by scanning the headlines and photo captions. Determine the specific time and place you will use the technique you chose.

The PhotoReading whole mind system is a tool with countless applications. You have just seen yourself experiencing some of them. Add another application to your reading repertoire in the next chapter.

A mystery writer PhotoRead dozens of mystery books to assimilate styles, techniques, dialogs, descriptions, etc. Immediately his writing flowed more easily. He began sending the first or second drafts of chapters to his agent instead of his usual fifth or sixth draft.

The technical director of the virtual reality department of a high-tech company PhotoRead all the literature he could find on his industry. He became a prolific writer, presenting professional papers to conferences around the country. He received high professional acclaim from his colleagues.

An actress is better able to memorize her lines by PhotoReading the script first. She also said this helps create a better understanding of her characters.

A university professor finds that PhotoReading techniques help her tremendously in selecting useful journal articles for her Ph.D. literature review, allowing her to sift quickly then concentrate on the relevant material.

9

Share Information Through Group Activation

I hear many business people complain about thick, ugly documents they encounter at work—specification manuals, requests for proposals, stacks of computer printouts, technical manuals for equipment, software manuals, and so on. I see these people's eyes sparkle with anticipation, if not amazement, when I suggest an alternative that involves PhotoReading.

When I first presented PhotoReading at IDS/American Express in Minneapolis, I worked with an information systems and data processing group. After a class session, several participants came up to me. The one holding a stack of reports said, "This seminar has been very interesting. But how do we use the techniques on *these?*" He dropped the stack on the table with a thud. Feeling a bit threatened, I told him we would cover applications of this sort during the next session.

That afternoon, I cleared my desk and took the first document— a blue covered, computer generated report—and set it in front of me. I read the front cover, which said "CATS Unscheduled Disbursements, Systems External Specifications." My brain instantly overloaded and blew a fuse. My heart started racing at the thought of teaching the next session. I could hear the ridicule and feel the humiliation. My palms got sweaty. No doubt about it, I was in document shock.

I numbly opened the front cover and tried to read the table of contents. Nothing made sense. It was all complete gibberish. Now my panic was complete.

Almost instinctively, I stopped everything, took in a deep breath, and dropped into the resource level of mind. I opened my eyes, entered PhotoFocus, and PhotoRead the report—once right side up, once upside down and backwards. After PhotoReading, I closed my eyes and gave myself the closing affirmation.

Then came the amazing part. I opened my eyes and looked at the table of contents again. Miraculously, everything made sense. I went on to postview the report and could clearly see the structure of the entire document, information covered, the purpose for it, and the conclusions drawn. I super read and dipped, and in minutes I knew exactly what data processing managers needed to know from it. Fantastic!

I bounced through the other documents like a kid in a candy store. It took me between 11 and 13 minutes to read any one of them well enough to understand and discuss it.

Imagine my confidence at the next session. I described how to read the reports using the PhotoReading whole mind system. One manager commented that I understood the reports better than he did, and his department generated similar documents quarterly.

 Reading stacks of business- or teacher-generated papers is simple using the PhotoReading whole mind system. If you need familiarity with a document, prior to a meeting or class, the strategy that follows is a winner.

Group activation

Say that you manage a group of three people, and that each of these people has differing degrees of expertise about what happens in your company as a whole. One person, for example, often works with the human resource department, another talks frequently to systems analysts in the data processing department, and the third person has responsibilities in marketing and product development.

One day you are handed the software manual for a new company-wide computer system. Looking at the table of contents, you find that you have six hundred pages of extra reading to complete in the next week. One option for handling this situation is the traditional one: you and each of your people slog through the manual from start to finish, releasing much hope of sleep for the next few nights.

Instead, try this: hand each of your staff a copy of the manual. Ask each of them to take the manual home for one night, preview it for a minute or two, and then spend another few minutes PhotoReading it before they go to sleep. During the next working day, meet as a group to activate and discuss the document.

In the meeting, go around the group and ask what they know from previewing the manual. This will insure everyone is starting from a similar frame of reference. Next, give your group an activation assignment. Ask each person to spend seven to ten minutes super reading and dipping in the manual to find specific information. Give them specific topics to focus on with specific questions related to areas of personal or professional interest.

For example, ask your human resource expert to super read and dip into the manual to judge how this new system will affect the company's need for new personnel or training programs. Ask your system's manager to judge the technical fit with existing systems, and so on.

After completing this assignment, the next step is to activate the manual in a group discussion. Have each person spend five minutes describing what he or she learned from activating the text. Let one person create a giant mind map that pools the main points described. Follow the mind mapping with an open discussion, allowing your employees to ask each other questions about the specific points they have made.

Experiment with this strategy, and you will be surprised at the richness and value of the ensuing discussion. As your employees ask and answer questions, they help each other activate the material they have read. In effect, this is PhotoReading followed by group activation.

Watching groups use this strategy, I have seen them reduce reading chores from several hours of wasted time to a matter of a few highly effective minutes. What's more, this process prompts people to share information across specialties—something that is surprisingly rare in the information age. The payoff is concrete: high-level people are freed from plowing through manuals for hours at a time; instead, they can return to what they do best. Groups turn into productive decision making forces, using shared information and learning to become even more effective as they go.

This is one of the most powerful tools I know about for coping with information overload and document shock. It is no longer feasible to expect any one person to master all the information on a given topic. Instead, use the PhotoReading whole mind system to create a regular process of sharing information across departments and areas of expertise.

Read
Entire
Section

If you wish to use this process in a structured way, the following format describes each step. Use it whenever several people need to share an understanding of a document.

1) Pre-Session Assignment

The beginning of the process includes a memo from the group leader with the reading assignment attached. The memo states the purpose and intended outcome of the meeting.

2) Individual Preparation

Complete the assigned reading in stages:

• Prepare (one minute).

• Preview the material (one to two minutes).

• PhotoRead (one to three minutes).

• Postview to discover two or three questions that might be relevant in the meeting.

• Optional: super read and dip to find answers to those questions (ten minutes maximum).

• Before sleep, visualize activating the materials and successfully accomplishing the group's outcome.

3) Group Activation

Restate the group's intent. Summarize the reading by describing the document in general terms, discussing the type of report or article, the main point of it, and questions the author addresses.

Next, assign the sections to be analyzed and the specific kind of analysis you want from each person. For example, one person could look at the report from the position of a management expert. One person could explore the problems raised. Another person could examine short range implications.

Ask each group member to rapid read the assigned section or super read and dip the entire text for the key ideas they are exploring. Remember to specify the time for completing the task. (Trained PhotoReaders generally activate a 15- to 30-page report in 7 to 12 minutes.)

4) Discussion—Analytical Format

Outline the structure and content of the entire document:

• List trigger words. What are their meanings? Do those meanings shift at any point in the text? (Refer back to Chapter 6 on postviewing for information on this.)

• List the main propositions. What ideas capture the opinion and facts presented in the document? Arrange these opinions and facts in a logical sequence to discover the key arguments. If you find the conclusion first, then look for the supporting reasons. If you find the reasons first, see where they lead.

• Examine the defined problems and the proposed solutions. What problems does the author solve? Are there any that remain unsolved?

• Critique the text. Discuss the merits and drawbacks of the ideas presented. What arguments do you agree with? What are the points of disagreement?

Discussion—Creative Format

Your group might choose to engage in a creative discussion instead of an analytical one. If that is the case, this format will be more appropriate.

• Describe your "feeling response" to the written materials. Keep in mind that feelings set a stage for how information will be interpreted.

• State the facts and information you have received from the text.

• Conduct a brainstorming session about the meaning, relationship, and relevance of this information to the group's outcome.

• Plan what to do about all this information, and establish the group's next step.

The benefits of the PhotoReading whole mind system can ripple throughout your organization and change the way you get things done at work. Shared decision-making occurs when everyone shares the same base of information. Using these techniques, individuals keep up with almost no effort or struggle.

A few minutes devoted to previewing and PhotoReading at night is not a major project. Taking ten minutes in a meeting to turn on the whole mind and activate relevant information with a strong purposeful approach to problem-solving is enormously productive. When sharing the activated information, the group is totally focused on decision-making.

Succeed in any group

Although this chapter has focused on business applications of group activation, you can use these skills whenever sharing information with others. Consider book clubs as an excellent opportunity to use and refine your PhotoReading skills. Community libraries and bookstores can often refer you to existing groups that welcome new members. If you cannot find one, start your own!

Many PhotoReaders attend study groups within their religious communities. Use the strategy outlined in this chapter to study scripture and discover how quickly you gain the benefits you seek. PhotoReading may be one of the best things for supporting your spiritual growth.

If you attend college classes, sooner or later you will find yourself in a group project where reading is involved. Use the techniques presented here to ensure you are always prepared. The other group members will recognize your leadership capabilities because of your amazing grasp of the information you study.

Another type of group, called success teams, are groups of three to five PhotoReaders who meet regularly to help each other accomplish personal and professional development objectives. It is a big commitment to meet every month to PhotoRead with others, but it has always paid off for those who have done it.

Get your group involved

How do you get your group members started today using PhotoReading? Buy copies of this book for them. Tell them to preview and PhotoRead the whole book, and then activate just this chapter. Do you think that will stimulate their curiosity?

Seriously, it is a good idea that everyone learns these skills. Tell them to use the guide at the beginning called "How to Read This Book" and read the book to Level 2. This is a one-hour investment. Consider purchasing the *PhotoReading Personal Learning Course*. In it I will guide you through learning the PhotoReading whole mind system. This book is included with the package.

Another way to get others involved is to bring a certified PhotoReading instructor into your company or community for a training course. Call Learning Strategies Corporation now for information on sponsoring in-company training.

You can say good-bye to worrying about how to contribute in meetings because you did not read the report. Gone are the nights of lugging papers home, only to ignore them, and then shamefully letting them pile up. Now you can stand up and take a powerful lead wherever you are. Information is power for those who know how to access it and share it in useful ways.

Simply do it. The demonstrations of success will happen. You can take specific steps to strengthen your application of these ideas in the next chapter.

Needing to learn French, a businesswoman PhotoRead the English/French dictionary repeatedly for two weeks before attending French classes at the Berlitz school in Brussels. Each night after class, she PhotoRead the course manuals and the dictionary. Within three days, she had advanced to the second book. School administrators told her she was performing two and a half times better than their previous best student.

An insurance salesman didn't have enough time to study for his exams, which have always been difficult for him. He used the PhotoReading whole mind system saying, "The worst that can happen is that I fail and have to retake the class." He passed.

An office manager said retrieving misfiled files became very easy. "I get into the state for PhotoReading, and the files seem to jump out of the drawer at me."

A bookkeeper said her ability to manipulate data in spreadsheets increased significantly. She found it easier to remember the programming commands and to detect errors.

A stay-at-home mom for 14 years learned PhotoReading as part of her plan to get back into the job market. She was soon hired by a medical technology company and got promoted four times. She attributes her skyrocketing career and her dream job to her new PhotoReading skills. At first she questioned her ability to even see the "blip page," but after PhotoReading 100 books in the first 30 days, even without activating, it became apparent to her. She began by PhotoReading job hunting and resume writing books to land a job as an administrative assistant. She moved on to database programming materials and was soon promoted to a clinical supervisor. Next she started PhotoReading people management books. She was then promoted to trial leader, so she began focusing on project management and team building books, as well as technical books about her company's products. In her new senior position she PhotoReads to stay current in her field. "Twenty percent of my success can be attributed to luck, 80 percent to PhotoReading. My income has shot up 200 percent!"

10

Enrich Your PhotoReading Experience

You become more skilled at PhotoReading when you put the techniques to work for you. Plain and simple: just do it. Unlike speed reading instructors that insist on endless repetition of perfunctory drills, PhotoReading instructors encourage taking relaxed, playful, and explorative interactions with reading materials. Doing so promotes fast, continuous skill development.

The concept of "no pain, no gain" is absurd when it comes to matters of the mind. You simply cannot become skilled at PhotoReading while beating yourself up. Using the steps of the PhotoReading whole mind system in all reading endeavors has proven to be the best route to building skills.

I also enrich my use of the system when I explore related areas of self-development. Discover for yourself that becoming more skilled with elements of PhotoReading actually improves the quality of your entire life.

The PhotoReading Whole Mind System leads to lovely benefits that extend well beyond improved reading speeds and comprehension. The same principles apply equally to approaching life with your whole mind. For example, PhotoReading improves concentration and memory, bringing greater pleasure in all your endeavors. Anything you set your mind to accomplish, you will learn faster and easier.

Let's explore specific ways to begin reaping the rich benefits available to you.

Cultivate the eye-mind connection

Extremely fast readers are visual readers. They rely on a direct connection between the eye and the brain. They do not need to subvocalize—that is, mentally hear the words on the page—in order to comprehend written materials. Studies indicate that subvocalizing is not critical to comprehension. Subvocalizing every word guarantees you can never read faster than the sound of your own voice can speak (about 220 words a minute is tops). Experiment with breaking your personal "sound" barrier. To learn this system well, push your speed, trusting that comprehension will indeed catch up.

Many of us have spent years developing a conflicting habit: receiving visual and auditory signals in order to understand our reading. Your brain most likely will not adjust to a total shift overnight. To encourage your development, relax when you read. Do not sweat the comprehension on the first or second pass through material. And, praise yourself for doing any and all techniques of the PhotoReading whole mind system.

Consider vision training

Any vision training strengthens your eyes and your brain's ability to process written information. Vision training I received included exercises for converging and diverging the eyes, accommodating my focus from far to near, tracking moving objects smoothly, expanding short-term visual memory storage, and enlarging my peripheral vision. Developing these skills results in a stronger, more balanced visual system. The payoff is tremendous efficiency in all visual tasks, especially reading.

Expand your peripheral awareness

Developing peripheral awareness involves looking at your visual field and noticing whatever is not in hard focus. The objective is to pull in information that usually eludes the conscious mind. The benefit is that information in this other 99 percent of the visual field can be attended to, and responded to, with remarkable efficiency.

Pupil dilation increases peripheral vision. This occurs naturally when light intensity decreases or when the eyes diverge, as in the PhotoFocus state. As an aid to this process, I recommend that you PhotoRead in warmer, softer light.

PhotoReading is designed to open our visual field. Like removing the "flight blinders" of a student pilot, practicing PhotoReading helps you notice more of what is there in front of you—for example, the edges of the book rather than a single word or word phrase.

The applications for increased peripheral awareness become limitless. With it, you increase your responsiveness to visual cues in the environment. For example, you can drive more defensively, increase your proficiency in sports such as racquetball and tennis, respond better when playing cards, sing in choirs with greater ease, function in a busy office environment more easily, find items in stores more quickly, and increase your typing speed.

Read Bullets

Here are some simple ways to work with peripheral awareness:

• When driving the car and looking down the road, notice the sides of the road, pick out movements in the side view mirrors, and read billboards without looking at them.

• Walk with a soft gaze, looking at a point on the horizon, and take in the wide panorama of the world around you.

• When in conversation, notice what items of clothing or jewelry people are wearing while looking only at their face.

• When PhotoReading, pay attention to the edges of the book or the spaces between the paragraphs.

• Work with a martial arts expert. The schools of Tai Chi and Aikido, which are considered the "softer" forms, are ideal.

• PhotoRead books that teach this kind of open, relaxed awareness. Books on Zen and meditation are excellent resources. The *Inner Game* books by Tim Gallwey describe many of the concepts of Zen meditation in an application-oriented, Westernized way. These books suggest many exercises that build skills related to PhotoReading.

After PhotoReading books on meditation and open awareness, do not activate them manually for a few days and notice what happens. Let your magnificent brain surprise and delight you with increased skills. Notice your experience and discover that magical moments become more commonplace as the quality of your life improves. See Chapter 13, "Discover Your Genius Potential with Direct Learning," for more insight into how this works.

Enter states of relaxed alertness

Decades of research show us that our best resources for learning and personal development are not available to us when we call on our conscious mind, the part that uses the five senses and focuses outwardly. An expanded range of brain resources are available as we change our state of conscious awareness to a more inward focus and rely on inner senses to understand the world. Using the expanded processing capabilities of the brain we can accelerate learning, improve sport performance, and enhance personal development.

You may know that the human brain produces an electrical frequency. The waves of electrical energy can be measured in Hertz (Hz) or cycles per second (cps) with a device known as an electroencephalograph (EEG). The brain normally operates in a range of frequencies from 1 to 30+ cycles per second (cps). Smaller frequency ranges within the normal range are associated with a variety of brain functions or capabilities.

Dr. F. Noah Gordon, in his book *Magical Classroom*, describes the smaller frequency ranges as "brain channels," similar to radio or television channels. At each frequency setting, different information is available to us. As with changing channels on the television, we can change our brain channels and access more of the brain's full potential.

The four channels are major states of awareness that are on call for each of us at all times. These channels are:

Channel 1—Action Channel (16-30 cps), associated with outward performance, critical thinking, and stress.

Channel 2—Relaxation Channel (12-15 cps), a stress-release gate opening inward to physically and mentally alert states.

Channel 3—Learning Channel (8-12 cps), the home of the real learner where we process new learning, associated with calm, effortless, relaxed inner awareness.

Channel 4—High Creativity/Pattern-Maker Channel (4-7 cps), the place of highest resources and super abilities, associated with reverie, intuition, creativity, and the genius self.

I have conducted numerous EEG measurements on PhotoReaders using a device called the Interactive Brainwave Visual Analyzer. A unique set of frequencies is reliably produced when someone enters PhotoFocus and PhotoReads a book. This characteristic "brain signature" appears almost instantaneously upon entering PhotoFocus, suggesting that the ideal brain state for PhotoReading may be linked more to the state of the eyes than to the physical relaxation of the body. However, those who learn to maintain states of relaxed alertness have the easiest time developing their PhotoReading skills.

Follow the instructions offered in Chapter 5 and enter the resource level of mind. Notice that you can change the quality of thinking and feeling at will. In turn, this state will influence your physiology such as the autonomic nervous system, heart rate, pupil dilation, perspiration, and adrenaline secretion. All these functions are controlled at the nonconscious level. This means that peaceful thoughts can register directly in the body.

It follows that when you are physically relaxed and mentally alert you have the most flexibility and control over the way you think and feel. Since learning is a process of changing the way you think and feel, learning can take place most easily at the resource level of mind.

To strengthen your skill at achieving relaxed alertness:

Read
Bullets

• Establish simple control over diet and exercise. A strong and well-nourished body and brain lead to a balanced and healthy mind. Eat low-fat, low-sugar foods. For PhotoReading, drink lots of water because water helps the blood carry oxygen to the brain.

• Take a moment now and then to breathe with deep inhalations and slow exhalations. Notice the relaxation and soothing feelings which flow comfortably through your body.

• Listen to Paraliminal CDs and other relaxing audio programs.

• PhotoRead relevant books on autogenic training, guided fantasy, Silva methods, meditation, and contemplative prayer. Remember, you do not have to activate every book in order for the concepts to benefit your life.

• Explore meditation. You will discover countless varieties, including Qigong, Yoga, and Zen. Many reputable teachers and centers throughout the world teach courses in meditation.

• Use Qigong (pronounced "chee gung"), the Chinese system of focused concentration and breathing. An excellent self-study course on Spring Forest Qigong techniques is available through Learning Strategies Corporation.

Use supportive Paraliminal sessions and Personal Learning Courses

A proven way to reinforce and enrich whole mind reading skills is with the use of audio programs that affirm your abilities to learn, relax, and establish new behaviors. Use them often.

I developed Paraliminal CDs, which combine progressive relaxation with the technology of neuro-linguistic programming (NLP). These CDs blend separate tracks of narration. One track is more analytical and "left-brained," guiding you in a step-by-step process to help you accomplish your goal. Another track is more "right-brained," using stories and symbolic imagery to reinforce the CD's central message.

Paraliminal CDs contain no subliminal messages and are not designed to induce hypnotic trances. Rather, they actually break the negative or self-limiting trances that have kept so many people stuck and unresourceful.

Several of these CDs are specifically designed to support the steps of the whole mind system.

Personal Genius helps you get into the flow state and use the full resources of your inner mind for learning.

Memory Supercharger gives you access to the vast memory storage of your whole brain. Use this CD before a presentation or exam to help you perform at your best.

Automatic Pilot helps you get into the flow state and move toward your goals without self-sabotage. This CD is great if you habitually talk yourself out of reading things you want or need.

Get Around To It helps eliminate procrastination and motivates you to take action now. If you find yourself putting off reading, then this CD can really help.

New Behavior Generator helps you establish the habit of reading and overcome resistance.

New History Generator helps you overcome a history of being a poor reader or of not being good at school.

Anxiety-Free helps you overcome anxieties around reading, taking tests, and taking responsibility for your own success.

Belief helps change limiting beliefs that may keep you from enjoying all the benefits of the PhotoReading whole mind system.

Dream Play helps you program and recall your dreams, which can be effective activation tools for PhotoReading.

Prosperity helps you enjoy the benefits of PhotoReading by attracting promotions, higher productivity, better grades, etc.

Deep Relaxation helps you access the PhotoReading state of relaxed alertness.

Self-Esteem Supercharger helps build a positive self-concept.

10-Minute Supercharger helps your mind become mentally alert and physically revitalized. It is great for long study sessions.

Establish outcomes; raise commitment

Having clear, well-formed goals is essential to achieving meaningful results in life. The brain is a goal-seeking device and must aim at a specific target in order to hit the mark. To achieve significant benefit from PhotoReading, continually set clear targets. Establish a purpose each time you read. Here are ways to support this activity:

• **Include a note on your daily "to do" list to use the PhotoReading whole mind system**. Integration of these skills happens as you apply them. Do not worry about practicing them; simply use them whenever you read. The word "practice" implies artificially created time to do something you have to do. Take the pressure off and just add this whole mind approach to handle your everyday reading priorities.

• **Set specific reading goals** and share them with a "PhotoReading buddy" who can review your progress. As you establish your purpose for reading, set yourself up to win. Rather than pressuring yourself with goals you think you "should" accomplish, set fun goals which represent what you truly want. Set goals which stretch your capabilities; at the same time, set goals you can reasonably accomplish.

• **If you do not get the results you want, go easy on yourself.** Keep playing with options. After all, if you always do what you've always done, you will always get what you've always gotten. Do things differently, confront old habits, and affirm your mind's potential.

• **Notice your progress.** Keep track of any concrete indicator of success in the direction of your goals. Let go of perfectionistic tendencies that expect only total success or complete failure. Celebrate all of your successes, no matter how small the step may be toward your end goal.

Use memory techniques

The "tip of the tongue" phenomenon is an example of knowing something but not being able to consciously articulate it. For many people, this is common with remembering names.

The best technique of letting information bubble up from the nonconscious mind into the conscious mind is to give yourself the space to remember. For example, tell yourself: "I know this person's name. His name is coming to me now." Then, dismiss the issue from your mind and allow your mind to retrieve it.

Consider this rule: *want* it to happen; *expect* it to happen; get out of the way and *let* it happen. This is the essence of a positive attitude toward yourself. It represents a basic trust that your mind is powerful and capable, ready to serve you whenever you want. A positive faith in the integrity of your mind is the cornerstone of successful whole mind reading.

Play with your dreams

The brain naturally uses dreams to process information that it received preconsciously. Noticing your dreams helps activate books you have PhotoRead because when you remember your dreams, you build a bridge to your conscious and nonconscious mind. In turn, this gives you more conscious access to the vast "data bank" of the brain.

Play with noticing your dreams. At first, simply remember your dreams when you awaken. As you do so, you may find yourself having lucid dreams—those in which you consciously respond to the events of your dream. The more frequently you remember dreams, and the clearer and more detailed your dream images, the more likely you are to have lucid dreams.

Motivation is key. For the most part, if you want to remember your dreams, you will. For many people, simply having the intention to remember and reminding themselves of this intention just before going to bed is enough.

To strengthen this resolve, keep pen and paper beside your bed, and create a mind map of your dreams every time you wake up. This activity helps you remember more dreams in the future.

Another method for remembering dreams is asking yourself each time you wake up: what was I just dreaming? This must be your first thought upon awakening; otherwise, you may forget some or all of the dream.

Be patient as you try to remember dreams. When you awaken in the morning, do not move or think of anything else. Pieces and fragments of the dream will come to you. Examine your thoughts and feelings as you lie in bed. This often provides the necessary cues for retrieving the entire dream. Keep at it, even if you recall nothing of your dreams at first.

I developed the *Dream Play* Paraliminal CD to aid in recalling dreams. You can also use this book as a springboard tonight. Much of this book is filled with information that will change the way you look at printed pages forever. This book can help you tap into the powerful reserves of your brain. Use it as one of the many tools at hand by PhotoReading it before you sleep.

Take the PhotoReading seminar

Enroll in a PhotoReading seminar. The seminar is different than the book in that you will be assisted by a professionally trained, Learning Strategies Corporation certified, PhotoReading instructor who uses special student course material published by us. Each instructor has guided the individual successes of many participants before you. Your individual needs and questions can be addressed as you think of them. More in-depth illustrations and examples are offered that meet your learning style. Plus, many experiences during the seminar cannot be fully described in book form. They bring rich meaning to the chapters you have read here.

In addition to learning the techniques, you will learn how to:

• PhotoRead and activate your brain to achieve your reading goals with higher comprehension.

• Reliably enter the resource level of mind in a matter of moments.

• Open your perceptual field to see with your mind what cannot be perceived by your eyes.

• Instantly balance the hemispheres of your brain with simple physical movement, thereby making reading more effective.

• Program your mind for new habit acquisition and help break the compulsion to read with inefficient reading techniques.

• Use your dreams as an activation technique.

• Make friends with your inner mind, trusting your intuitive guidance to solve problems using the vast database of your nonconscious reserves of mind.

The biggest advantage to attending an intensive seminar setting is the power of doing something and getting feedback. During the seminar, you will PhotoRead and activate books using all the techniques described in this book. We even teach you how to PhotoRead a dictionary, think of a word, and know where it is on the page.

When you meet others with like-minded attitudes in a course, you gain the support needed to get you through the stages of learning. You may even find some new friends in the process.

Periodically I lead the PhotoReading Retreat. Look for dates and more information on our website, www.LearningStrategies.com/PhotoReading.

Use the PhotoReading Personal Learning Course

I had never enjoyed learning from "self-study" programs. So, when it came time for me to produce one, it had to be one I wanted to hear. After 18 months of development, the *PhotoReading Personal Learning Course* was ready to ship to our eager customers. It turned out to be a smash hit.

I received a call from the human resources director at a large Minnesota business who asked, "Would you be open to some feedback on your course." I gulped once and said, "Sure."

Dreading the worst, I was amazed at the praise he lavished upon me. "I wanted to let you know this is the best audio learning program I have ever used, and I've owned a lot of them. Congratulations on excellent work." I sighed in relief.

"You would never get me into a seminar," he said. "I'm just not comfortable with the typical level of self-disclosure involved in public programs. Your self-study program gave me tremendous permission to proceed at my own rate, with explicit decision points to go on or stop. I finished the entire program in five days by spending a few hours each afternoon, I figured a total of 15 hours."

I felt sincerely acknowledged. The diligent work of the great crew that helped me put the program together had paid off.

While nothing substitutes for the power of the live seminar, the *PhotoReading Personal Learning Course* is an excellent alternative when someone cannot attend the PhotoReading seminar.

Throughout this book I have encouraged you to read other books, enroll in the PhotoReading seminar or use the self-study course, and listen to supportive audio programs such as my Paraliminals. I do this because the more information you have, the more accomplished you will be in truly using the innate talents you possess. Explore the benefits you can achieve using our programs listed at the back of this book.

Be free to discover what author Peter Kline calls "the everyday genius" within you. I cannot convince anyone that they possess genius talents. Each person must find this truth within. My sincere wish is that you discover this truth for yourself.

As you strengthen your eye-mind connection, expand peripheral awareness, cultivate powerful mental states, and remember your dreams, you will deepen and expand your skills at PhotoReading. You will experience the culmination of your new skills as you discover syntopic reading in Chapter 11.

A Systems Manager for the United States Air force used PhotoReading to get his degree in Computer Information Systems Management. He took 15 credit hours worth of exams in humanities, social sciences, and world religions within one week, having never attended classes on the subject matter. To graduate he had to pass these tests, so his motivation was high. He PhotoRead six books on each topic a couple days before each exam. Not only did he pass and get 15 credit hours, he got a B-plus average on the exams. This score was higher than the average of the students who took the exams after attending a semester of classes. He is now using PhotoReading to earn a commission as an officer.

A college senior used PhotoReading to prepare for his final exams. As a senior working to secure a job for after graduation, he dropped his regular studies hoping to get caught up at the minute. He phoned a PhotoReading coach at Learning Strategies Corporation in a panic the night before the exams. After the conversation, he got into a relaxed state and PhotoRead his class materials. He ate dinner, worked out, and went to bed relaxed. The next day he confidently took his exams and passed. PhotoReading put him at ease and allowed him to prepare mentally for the tests.

Before giving a presentation on peripheral development to a technical college supervisory management team, an instructor PhotoRead ten background books. She activated the books using syntopic reading strategies. The presentation went so well that the management team invited her to return as the subject matter expert for another presentation.

11

Use Syntopic Reading for Lifelong Exploration

My professor in graduate school told the class to pick a subject in the field of human resource management. "Go read all the books you can find on the subject and write a 10- to 20-page report on what you learn."

I found 12 books. Using the PhotoReading whole mind system I finished all the books and completed a mind map of my report—all in one afternoon. I wrote the report from the mind map and turned it in.

When the paper was returned to me it had only two marks on it: "100%" and "Excellent!" Never before in my undergraduate or graduate work had such a project ever been so easy.

My colleague Patricia Danielson, whose early contributions to PhotoReading led me to call her co-developer, refined the idea into an exercise called "syntopic reading." She originally tested it in Europe, and it proved wildly successful.

The syntopic reading exercise enriches the learning of PhotoReading. To syntopically read, you must draw upon all the skills you have developed and go to the next level of mastery.

Imagine reading three to five books on a subject in just one afternoon. You can with the basic steps of syntopic reading described in this chapter.

How it works

Let us say you have an interest in a subject and find a book you really want to read. By PhotoReading and activating three additional books on the same subject, you can know the one book better. But here is the best news: it takes less time to apply our system to all four books than it takes to read one using your old reading techniques.

Think of reading as a path of lifelong exploration. As we follow this path, we soon discover there are opposing viewpoints on every significant topic. For the skilled reader, differing views create a tension that invites the next level of resolution. Syntopic reading provides a new vantage point and an easy route to the synthesis of existing viewpoints.

People who read well understand many sides of a topic and come to their own conclusions. Syntopic reading ensures that more of your ideas are based on your own thinking. This is done by exposing yourself to various viewpoints and choosing or constructing one that ultimately rings true for you. Your truth comes from your reasoning, overall knowledge, and reflection on experience—and not just from the last book you read. Often, in fact, you must read several books on the same subject to gain a deeper understanding.

The experience of one PhotoReading student demonstrated how easily she gained the advantages of reading multiple books on a subject. She had returned to school 25 years after high school to get her college degree in a local community college. Prior to taking an essay exam in her history class, she PhotoRead seven books relating to the subject she was studying.

She beamed as she described to me how the words flowed during the exam. She had never felt so relaxed and confident during an essay exam, and she proudly added, "I got an A on the exam!" She had naturally found the transition from PhotoReading to syntopic reading.

Syntopic reading was first described fifty years ago in Mortimer Adler and Charles Van Doren's classic text *How to Read a Book*. Adler considered the thinking skills used in syntopic reading to be the ultimate goal of a well-read person. We added the skills of the PhotoReading whole mind system to syntopic reading to help synthesize ideas more efficiently.

One man in a class of mine was in a university doctoral program in education. Writing papers had always been a time-consuming problem for him. He would have to read several books, distill the information, generate his own ideas, and write the paper. After learning syntopic reading, he applied his skills to writing papers. He called me several months later. "This is unbelievable!" he exclaimed. "I cannot tell you how easy PhotoReading has made it for me. I can finish, in one afternoon, a paper that used to take me two or three days."

How can it be? It is all in the basic steps of whole mind syntopic reading that follow:

1) Establish a purpose

The first active step of syntopic reading is to state a purpose that has meaning and value for you.

Be clear and specific—it is crucial. Suppose your purpose is to learn money management strategies. An effective purpose statement could be:

Optional: Read through all 10 steps

"I want to learn effective methods to save money and invest wisely so I can build my financial independence."

That statement is clear and specifies a purpose with personal meaning. Meaning also increases long-term retention. Notice how much more power it has than a broader statement like "I want to learn more about financial planning."

2) Create a bibliography

The second active step is to create a bibliography—a list of books that you plan to read. Preview your books to determine if they fit your purpose. For this exercise, choose nonfiction books by different authors on a subject that you really want to understand.

3) PhotoRead all materials the day before activating

The mind needs incubation time to create new connections. PhotoRead your selected books the day before you plan to activate them. PhotoReading makes the difference in your ability to process ideas at high speeds. During sleep, your brain finds ways to categorize information exposed to it during PhotoReading.

4) Create a giant mind map

Take out your books, a large sheet of paper, and colored markers for mind mapping. Use mind mapping for making notes during the remaining steps of syntopic reading. Look at the chart shown as a suggestion for how to organize your mind map. Your initial statement of purpose takes a prominent place in the center of your sheet of

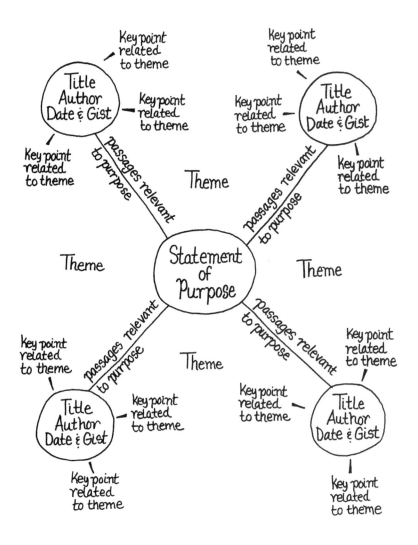

(Write the words about the major themes and concepts around the edges. These are your own words to describe the topic as a whole.)

paper. Leave enough room to revise your purpose statement later if you desire. The purpose statement in the center will help remind you that your mind map is about your purpose, not about the books. Use it to capture material from all the books that speak to your purpose. The content of any individual book takes less priority over the importance of your purpose.

5) Find relevant passages

Super read and dip through each of the books finding passages relevant to your purpose. In this step, your purpose reigns supreme over the purposes of the authors. The reason for holding your purpose as the guiding light is to pull out the otherwise obscure passages that can serve your purpose. Continue mind mapping the passages you find.

Let go of your desire to read in too much detail at this point. Use only light dipping throughout the books, and restrict your dipping to relevant passages. You may find during this step that your purpose statement will be refined as the complexities of the topic become clearer.

Think of this as a discussion with the authors of these books. Imagine these authors sitting around in a circle with you. Ask them a question and let them speak to your purpose. The objective is not to understand their books; it is to understand your purpose.

6) Summarize in your own words

If you step back and look at your mind map, you will notice a number of important concepts being addressed. Briefly summarize what you think about the subject so far.

It helps to create neutral, jargon-free terminology of your own. Different authors may use different words to say the same things. Finding a neutral set of terms creates meaningful associations and makes the concepts your own.

7) Discover themes

Explore your mind map and your books for similarities and differences among the various authors' viewpoints. When you reach this stage, you will begin to uncover the central themes that all or most of the authors are attempting to address. Make note of these.

8) Define the issues

When authors have opposing viewpoints, these differences are points of contention or issues. Uncover differing viewpoints, and you will enhance your knowledge about the subject.

In this step, you super read and dip to find key points related to these issues. Picture yourself as an investigative reporter in a room with your authors. Pose the central questions to each of them.

Go quickly from one book to another, answering one question at a time. As soon as you find it in one book, leave that book and start flipping through the next one.

9) Formulate your own view

As you discover issues and explore various viewpoints, you automatically begin to synthesize your own viewpoint. Look at all sides and take no sides at first. Make a deliberate effort to remain objective and avoid being partial in your analysis.

After gathering enough information, create your own position. Formulate your own opinion based on your research.

10) Apply

After choosing your position on the subject, you must create an argument to support your view, based on specific information from your books.

Order the key issues in such a way as to throw more light on the subject. Be specific in creating any argument for your position. To add credibility to your argument you should be prepared to quote your sources. In this case, it helps to always accompany a statement of an author's view with an actual quotation from the text, referenced by the page number. Create another mind map of your viewpoint before writing a formal report. This saves time and helps you present your ideas clearly.

Most business people and students fulfill their needs by the end of the previous step. That may be as far as they want to go with their subject. But for the person writing a college-level paper or detailed business report, this additional step is important.

How much time do you expect to invest in syntopic reading? We suggest you take only two 45-minute periods for activation. That is all. The investment before is approximately 10 to 15 minutes per book to quickly preview, PhotoRead, and postview. When finished, most participants recognize that they have achieved 80 to 90 percent of what they really want and need.

When you syntopically read three to five books, you may find one worthy of further study, one that seems to capture the subject most concisely. If you are interested, complete your study of that book using the activation steps of the PhotoReading whole mind system. Perhaps a quick rapid read will be sufficient to gather the remaining information you need. Depending upon the subject and the book, you might finish this in twenty minutes or four hours.

The cumulative power of syntopic reading

When you look at all the authors listed in the bibliography to this book, you will see that these are sources from my syntopic reading. Similarly, the PhotoReading seminar is a product of examining many authors and many researchers. Many authors cited here also referenced many authors—sometimes fifty to one hundred different books and journals.

Every time you syntopically read, you have the accumulated mental energies of hundreds of thinkers with thousands upon thousands of hours of labor and experience backing you in achieving your purpose. When you feel the power of this, you really understand the thrill of syntopic reading. Since you choose the unique combination of authors, you may stumble on a new point of view that has not been considered by anyone.

Patricia Danielson reported a stunning example of one of her students. A physician from Brussels used syntopic reading in his field of homeopathy. Every quarter, a number of homeopathic physicians from across Europe gather to share research papers. In preparation for a presentation, he syntopically read and mind mapped the major textbooks of homeopathy. When he looked at his mind maps, they seemed nonsensical. He put them in a file for later review.

Two months later, he pulled out his mind maps and laid them on the floor. Amazingly, they all made total sense to him. In fact, the new ideas that came to him were revolutionary. He quickly prepared his paper and a few weeks later presented it at the quarterly meeting.

Doctors at the meeting were astounded with the insights this man had revealed. One doctor commented that never in twenty years had he made the connections explained in this presentation. When the assembly inquired how the PhotoReader had made such leaps in his thinking, he described the PhotoReading process and syntopic reading. The next PhotoReading seminar in Brussels had seven of those doctors in attendance.

Visualize the process

Take a moment to integrate the ten steps of syntopic reading with a quick visualization. Think of a subject that you would like to study. What purpose do you desire to fulfill? Imagine going to the library and selecting a dozen books on the subject. Briefly look them over to determine which three to five you will take home with you. These are the ones you feel will meet your purpose.

Imagine that evening, previewing and PhotoReading the books. The next day you awaken raring to go. You create a giant mind map, establishing a clear purpose statement and writing it at the center of the mind map.

Super read and dip to find relevant passages and mind map these. As you notice patterns emerging, add a list of your own terms around the border of your map to summarize your findings. Explore the themes being addressed. Mind map these along with significant points of view that relate to issues of contention between authors. Remember, your objective is not to figure out the books. Your objective is to fulfill your purpose.

Feel the cumulative power of all this information. It is as if the authors were all present, speaking to your purpose. Imagine applying the valuable insights you gain in a most meaningful way for you. As you conclude your visualization, experience the thrill of syntopic reading.

A company CEO uses syntopic PhotoReading to great success, completing four books in just 60 minutes. "I feel confident that any subject I need to tackle can be dealt with using syntopic reading."

12

Questions and Answers for the Beginning PhotoReader

Simply knowing about the component skills and techniques of the PhotoReading whole mind system is not enough. You must develop and use the skills in real life. That is when questions arise.

The most common question asks, "Am I doing it right?" To know the answer with certainty, follow the instructions for each step you perform. The instructions found in this book have been developed, refined, and explained to hundreds of thousands of people before you. If you have doubts about any of the steps, reread the chapter and closely follow the instructions again.

Each step of the PhotoReading whole mind system produces an effect when you use it. For example, when you have previewed a business report, within 2-3 minutes you will know the structure and format of the report, the key points being covered, and whether investing any more time in it will be worthwhile to you. Did you achieve the results you expected with the technique? If not, there is a good reason.

We have found that occasionally a course participant will read or hear one thing, think another, and perform it differently than either. Are you performing the steps as explained in the instructions? Even if you do not achieve your final goal with a single technique, you will most likely receive indicators that you are on track and moving in the direction of your goal. Pay close attention to any concrete indicator of success, no matter how small it may be. This will quickly reassure you that you are on track.

If you have followed instructions and produce conflicting results, then your approach to the task could be throwing you off course. In the following sections of this chapter we explore how to ensure you maintain the ideal mindset during the use of the PhotoReading whole mind system. Use the ideas presented here, and you will charge ahead with confidence and success.

How can I quickly learn to use PhotoReading?

Since the ninth grade, you have been able to recognize words instantly, without having to sound them out. You are already well-versed in the exquisite array of visual patterns that we call written words. Why then do you feel compelled to sound out every word? Learning to read installed a set of training wheels that may have never come off. PhotoReading not only removes them; it helps install rockets in their place.

Learning a new skill will confront years of established habitual behavior. You need to go easy on yourself. Learning can be frustrating, especially if you have gremlins.

Gremlins are habits and disempowering beliefs that create negative feelings and stop us from learning. They are worrisome little creatures according to Richard Carson in his book *Taming Your Gremlin*.

How do you deal with gremlins? If you try to exterminate them, says Carson, they only get bigger. Instead, play with them. Love them to death. More specifically, call to mind the "NOPS" formula: Notice it, Own it, Play with it, Stay with it. With NOPS, any frustration you may feel can be easier to handle and need not become an obstacle to further learning.

N—Notice your feelings. Feelings are not right or wrong; they just are.

O—Own your experience. Admit any frustration. Problems we openly acknowledge are solvable; those we deny will only continue.

You can call up many comforting thoughts whenever you feel frustrated with learning. Take a new twist on an old saying: if at first you don't succeed, you are normal. So do it again.

P—Play with your experience. Push into the tailspin and see what happens. Go deeper into your confusion. Ask yourself questions. Doing so may lead to even greater confusion at first. Be childlike—it is okay to learn.

S—Stay with it. Too often we interpret frustration as a sign to give up. Instead, see this emotion as an invitation to forge ahead. If you do, you will start producing new results from reading.

With NOPS in mind, learning the PhotoReading whole mind system is a fast and gentle experience. It helps you enter the mindset of a child learning to walk. Falling down is not a time for self-castigation or public humiliation. It is a signal to get up, adjust your approach, and try again. Using the NOPS formula, you can be your best cheerleader and quickly master the skills.

How can I measure my performance during the PhotoReading step?

When it comes to the PhotoReading step, assessing your performance must be done in a nontraditional way, because during this step the goal is to keep conscious interference to a minimum. If you ask yourself while PhotoReading, "Am I doing this correctly?" it is already too late. You are not.

This is the same dilemma created when asking a sleeping person "Are you sleeping?" The very act of inquiring immediately pulls the subject out of the experience in which he is engaged. Not only does that stop one's involvement in the activity, it also negatively influences the outcome of the very experiment being performed.

When the mind studies the mind, a traditional experimental model does not work. Any experiment where the experimenter (or observer) is also the subject will be contaminated. The mind will always influence the outcome of its own experiment. So, if you are PhotoReading and wondering if you are doing it correctly, you cannot be. PhotoReading requires that you immerse yourself in the flow of the experience, so that the act of PhotoReading occurs without self-conscious or self-critical awareness.

To study the effectiveness of your PhotoReading, stay in the flow as you PhotoRead. Afterward, think back on your experience and consider:

• Did I relax physically and mentally and enter the resource level of mind?

• Did I affirm my concentration and purpose?

• Did I maintain a steady state with relaxed breathing, rhythmic page turning, and a chant in my conscious mind?

• Did I maintain PhotoFocus, either with the blip page or with awareness of the four corners and the white space on the page?

• Did I state my closing affirmations?

If you can answer yes, then you did the PhotoReading step correctly. To examine the effects of PhotoReading, you must perform a test of some kind after the fact. Such tests can be subjective or objective. Throughout this book, I have printed the stories given us by PhotoReaders from around the world. Their experiences can serve as examples of tests you might perform on yourself. Other tests that have helped many people demonstrate the immediate effects of the PhotoReading technique can be found at the end of Chapter 7.

During the early stages of learning the PhotoReading whole mind system, I recommend you step up to challenges in which you feel you can win. Build your confidence and take on even bigger challenges. If you do not feel ready to perform a test on television like the one described next, pick one that works for you.

A PhotoReader in Germany was asked to appear as a test subject for a news story about the PhotoReading whole mind system. Under the watchful eyes of the interviewer, production crew, and camera, she selected a book from several offered. She previewed, PhotoRead, and formulated questions. The next day she activated with super reading, dipping, and mind mapping, spending a total of 45 minutes with the book. She was then asked, while on camera, specific questions on the book. She answered every one correctly.

When lecturing in Munich, I showed a video of the five-minute television story and had the PhotoReader speak to the group about her experience. She said, "I never believed I could have done that. But when asked, I realized I faced an important decision: either I could live the rest of my life believing I could not perform successfully, or, I could take the challenge and find out the truth." Interestingly, a man from the audience said it was too unbelievable to imagine that *he* could ever do such a thing. Unfortunately, if he maintains that mindset he never will.

Can anyone learn to PhotoRead?

We have taught PhotoReading in dozens of countries, in many languages, to people from ages 9 to 93 who came with very diverse backgrounds and reading abilities. The secret to success in every case rests in the mindset or attitude of the learner. The attitude to maintain is one that is determined, persistent, and patient. This mindset has been beautifully described throughout the ages as the "beginner's mind." It helps us into a new paradigm of reading.

One of the great traps we face as PhotoReaders comes from already knowing how to read. Our previous training gives us certain notions about acceptable speed and levels of comprehension. Then along comes PhotoReading which asks us to change how we approach our reading problems.

Only a completely new paradigm will help see us through the pressures of deadlines and paper blizzards. Sometimes I hear beginning PhotoReaders say, "This is totally redefining what it means to read."

Maintaining the beginner's mind takes us to a place where we can glimpse new options. This concept goes back to the ancient school of Zen Buddhism. Shunryu Suzuki, a Zen master, said, "In the beginner's mind there are many possibilities, but in the expert's there are few." And he added: "We must have a beginner's mind, free from possessing anything, a mind that knows everything is in flowing change. Nothing exists but momentarily in its present form…"

Today we live in a world that requires us to become beginners over and over again in the face of impermanence, continuous change, and chaos. Re-examining what we have been taught about reading is just one example of the need for beginner's mind, and the dizzying pace of change guarantees that we will see more.

You do not have to study Zen to learn PhotoReading. There is a place for rules and for being the expert. There is also a place for questioning everything. PhotoReaders have both attitudes. We honor the conscious, rational mind, with its ability to set goals. We also acknowledge and use the expanded capabilities of the brain with its ability to find creative ways to reach our goals.

Using PhotoReading, you keep your present reading skills and gain new options. You not only win a new relationship with the printed word, you also find out how to respond when the world changes at a hectic pace. As an adult with a beginner's mind, you will rediscover the joy of continual learning.

How long will it take to learn this system?

As an automobile driver, I found learning to pilot an airplane both familiar and strange. A reader learning PhotoReading experiences similarities and radical differences to regular reading. It takes less time to learn the familiar and more time to learn the strange.

There are four stages to learning anything that is different or unusual. The length of time it takes will depend on how you move through the stages of learning. Let me illustrate each stage as it applies to learning PhotoReading.

In the first stage, you notice piles of unread material and feel a pervasive sense of information anxiety. Even so, you do not recognize the source of this problem, let alone how to respond. Something in your life is broken, but you are not aware of what needs fixing.

At this level it is common to feel fear, sometimes paired with excitement over the possibility of solving the problem. Label this step **Unconscious Incompetence.**

Next, you sense that your present reading habits are not serving you well. Those habits, in fact, are a major source of information anxiety. You learn about PhotoReading and even try some of the techniques. These techniques seem unfamiliar. Now you know what is broken, you know what to do, but you are unable to do it yet. Label this stage **Conscious Incompetence.**

The third stage represents a quantum leap. You use PhotoReading skills and experience success with them. Even so, these skills are not fully integrated into your life. You still need to remind yourself to use this new approach with written materials. Label this level **Conscious Competence.**

Finally, you enter the stage of mastery. Now PhotoReading is so familiar to you that you use it automatically. The techniques become as natural as breathing. You experience not only a new relationship with the printed word but a new quality of life. You reduce or eliminate those unread piles and continually satisfy your purpose for reading. Label this stage **Excellence**.

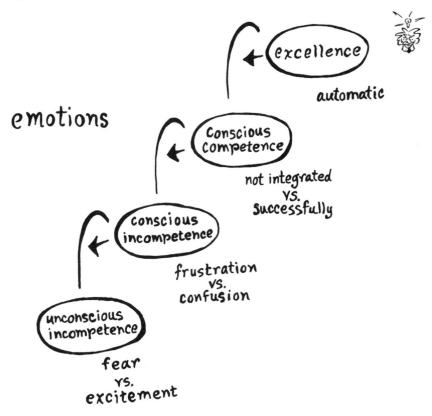

emotions

excellence
automatic

Conscious Competence
not integrated vs. successfully

conscious incompetence
frustration vs. confusion

unconscious incompetence
fear vs. excitement

Learning means passing though the stage of consciously realizing our incompetence—knowing that we do not know something important or that we lack a desired skill. Not surprisingly, certain emotions often accompany this discovery: confusion, frustration, fear, and anxiety.

My suggestion is simple: love it all. No matter what comes up for you as you learn PhotoReading, embrace it. No emotion you experience is wrong, and all your feelings serve a purpose. Confusion can create curiosity. Chaos can lead to clarity.

When I teach PhotoReading seminars at Learning Strategies Corporation, I love hearing people move through such feelings. When people say they are confused, I cheer. When they say they are frustrated, I quickly do what I can to move them into confusion. Behind this apparent craziness is a key insight: confusion is one step we climb on the way to excellence. Confusion signals that people are committing an act of learning.

In contrast, approaching problems with a sense of certainty and an unwillingness to let go of old beliefs leads to frustration. We get stuck in a state of learned helplessness, a state of not knowing. These two paths are summarized in the following diagram:

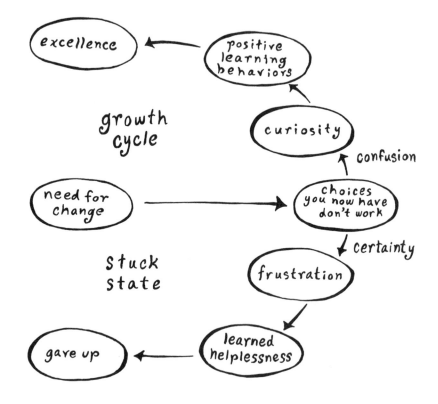

Unfortunately, our education often leads us down the path of frustration. In the traditional educational model of reading, confusion equals failure, and frustration equals incompetence. For some, joy in reading never appears and learning stops.

Whatever feelings you experience while learning PhotoReading are fine. Do not suppress any emotional state, any degree of confusion. You may be tempted to compare yourself with others: "I am not doing this right. Everybody else can do this. Why can't I?" If you detect such thoughts, let them come to full awareness and be willing to let them go. Remind yourself that conscious competence is coming your way.

Reading gets right to the heart of self-image. Our self-concept is often bound up with our success as learners, and much of our experience with learning ties to reading. I find that people label themselves as poor readers too readily and thus feel ineffective. Such frustration quickly tarnishes our self-image.

The alternative is to accept the emotional ups and downs of learning, to see them as a natural and graceful dance. If you do, you will shorten the path to excellence.

What state of mind should I be in when using the PhotoReading whole mind system?

Think about times when you have been absolutely absorbed in reading. It is important for us to explore those experiences in more depth, because, at those moments, you are transformed into a skilled, powerful reader—effortlessly.

Remember what those times were like. Perhaps you were engrossed in a novel. Maybe you were savoring a love letter. Or perhaps you were solving a murder mystery. In any case, a curious thing happened: you were unaware of anything else going on around you. It was as if the pictures, images, and feelings inside you were more important than the book in front of you. You were no longer reading words—you had stepped into another reality. What was going on behind your eyes was far more important than what appeared in front of them.

People describe these experiences with remarkably similar language. "I lost all track of time and place." "I was not conscious of words on a page." "I was just seeing movies in my mind." "I absorbed the words without effort." "Words just flowed from the page to my mind."

Flow—that is a handy word for it. It captures the key features of the experience: ease, fluidity, lack of effort, absorption, concentration, softness, relaxation, efficiency, and enhanced productivity.

Although this experience sounds like an altered state of consciousness, it is not abnormal. Human beings have known about the "flow experience" for hundreds

> Stephen Mitchell, a translator of the Tao, describes the flow state: A good athlete can enter a state of body-awareness in which the right stroke or the right movement happens by itself, effortlessly, without any interference of the conscious will. This is a paradigm for non-action: the purest and most effective form of action. The game plays the game; the poem writes the poem; we can't tell the dancer from the dance.

of years, using a variety of terms to describe it. The *Tao Te Ching*, a spiritual text from China by Lao Tsu, speaks of effortless action, or nonaction. Psychologist Abraham Maslow spoke of "peak experiences," describing them in a similar way.

Mihaly Csikszentmihalyi, a psychologist from the University of Chicago, revealed that flow experiences can happen to anyone. His studies of this state have included clerks, assembly-line workers, athletes, engineers, and managers. He says flow states bear a strong resemblance to other well-known phenomena—hypnosis and meditation.

Ah, but if we could only flip a switch and enter that flow state whenever we read. We would be in states of deep attention, free of effort or strain, working smoothly, quickly, and efficiently. We would be relaxed, active, and alert, all at the same time. Reading would be a breeze—as easy to flow through technical information as a novel.

The PhotoReading whole mind system is that switch. The flow state is your birthright, one of your potentials as a human being. Through PhotoReading, you get a chance to choose this experience instead of leaving it to chance. This state is not a fluke or some kind of out-of-body experience. Rather, it is a naturally occurring event, and the secret is to make it habitual during all your reading.

What do accelerative learning and PhotoReading have in common?

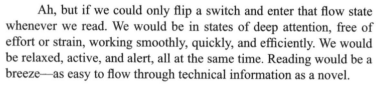

As a child, you naturally used strategies of accelerative learning to accomplish the monumental tasks of learning to walk and talk. Nothing you learn as an adult will equal the complexity of those tasks.

The skills of accelerative learning are still with you from childhood, obscured as they might be from years of abuse, misuse, and disuse. You simply need to reawaken your mastery and apply it to the task of reading. The PhotoReading whole mind system draws heavily from accelerative learning, making it easy and fun to learn and use.

One of the best-known researchers in the study of accelerative learning is Georgi Lozanov, a Bulgarian psychologist. Dr. Lozanov has written many papers supporting the claim that we use barely 10 percent of our brain capacity. He and his staff of researchers believe that we can systematically learn to tap the hidden reserves—the other 90 percent—of the mind. He developed his findings into an applied system for learning.

Lozanov's methods allow both hemispheres of the brain to work together as an orchestrated team. When that happens, our capacity to learn increases exponentially.

Lozanov claimed you can expose yourself to vast amounts of information, absorb it effortlessly, and use it when you need it. Those are precisely the skills you need to survive in the age of information overload and document shock.

At the heart of Lozanov's learning methods are three steps: *decode*, *concert*, and *activate*. These steps parallel the PhotoReading whole mind system.

Decoding is a "once over lightly"—a quick overview of the material to be learned.

During the concert session, learners enter a state of relaxed alertness to receive a more complete exposure to the material. This information is often presented as a story or play and accompanied by classical music playing in the background.

Finally, learners activate the material, that is, call it to the conscious mind and apply it. Instead of drill sessions and rote memorization, activation uses group discussion, games, skits, and other nontraditional methods.

See the connection? Lozanov's decode-concert-activate is our preview-PhotoRead-activate. The PhotoReading whole mind system incorporates many aspects of Lozanov's methods as does the teaching of the PhotoReading seminar.

I know I rely too heavily on my conscious rational mind. What else can I do?

Read
Bullets

In the early 1980s, Howard Gardner, a Harvard psychologist, developed an idea that complements Lozanov's work. Gardner said that our schooling works mostly on two kinds of intelligence: one that involves language and one that involves logic. Gardner concluded that this was only a small part of the picture, however. A more accurate view of intelligence includes all eight of the following capacities:

• Linguistic Intelligence—the ability to skillfully describe the world with words.

• Logical-Mathematical Intelligence—the ability to represent the world with numeric symbols and manipulate those symbols according to the rules of logic.

- Musical Intelligence—the ability to appreciate and use the nonverbal "language" of melody, rhythm, harmony, and tone color.

- Spatial Intelligence—the ability to perceive the visual world accurately and recreate it in the mind or on paper.

- Bodily-Kinesthetic Intelligence—the ability to use the body for skilled self-expression or as a tool for learning.

- Interpersonal Intelligence—the ability to perceive and understand other people's feelings and desires.

- Intrapersonal Intelligence—the ability to clarify personal values and gain insight through solitude.

- Naturalist Intelligence—the ability to see patterns anddistinguish and classify things in the natural world.

Read Bullets

Think of a time you learned something masterfully. Consider which of the eight intelligences you used. You already know how to excel at learning and can do so again at any time. Use the strengths you already possess.

Imagine applying all eight intelligences plus intuition to your reading. The PhotoReading whole mind system helps you do exactly that. All your intelligences are invited to the act of reading. In this sense, PhotoReading is not a reading program but a learning program—a set of strategies for learning anything. Anything.

How does activation tap into the expanded processing capabilities of the brain?

According to Dr. Win Wenger, author of *The Einstein Factor*, the nonconscious storage capacity of the brain exceeds the capacity of the conscious mind by ten billion to one. These are the reserves of the mind that you draw from during activation.

An example of activation is the tip of the tongue phenomenon that often takes place in remembering names. You know the scene: you see a familiar person at a party, but his or her name slips your mind. You try for a minute to recall the name. This stimulates the neural circuitry of your brain. Then, a few minutes later, the name suddenly flashes in your mind, often while you are talking to someone else and not consciously trying to remember it. Your brain generated the name based on the stimulation of neural pathways established when you first learned the person's name.

Activation can also take place on a grander scale. A writer I know practices meditation, which is another way of entering the state of relaxed alertness we cultivate in PhotoReading. He says that some of his best ideas come during periods of meditation, particularly when he is struggling with the content or structure of a manuscript. Frequently, outlines for entire books come to him in this way.

Artists of all types describe similar events in their lives. Aaron Copland, the distinguished American composer, said that writing music begins with transcribing themes that blossom spontaneously from within. As he put it in *What to Listen for in Music*:

> The composer starts with his theme, and the theme is a gift from Heaven. He doesn't know where it comes from—has no control over it. It comes almost like automatic writing. That is why he keeps a book very often and writes themes down whenever they come.

You do not have to be a great composer or writer to draw on these deep, creative reserves. You need a relaxed alertness along with a gentle request for the ideas you seek to surface in the conscious mind.

This has profound implications. The secret is to get out of the way and let yourself PhotoRead.

Will hard work help me develop my skills?

PhotoReading may seem like a bundle of paradoxes, because it is. Think about what I am suggesting: to get more out of your reading, spend less time with it; to gain more information, do not worry about conscious comprehension; to succeed at reading, quit trying so hard and start playing; and to get what you want, let go of your need for results.

During one seminar I met a woman who understood perfectly the paradoxical nature of PhotoReading. Soon after we began PhotoReading books, the number of her correct answers on comprehension tests climbed into the 90 percent range and stayed there. I asked her how that happened. "I simply decided up front that I have nothing to prove. If the techniques work, fine. If they don't, fine. For me the important thing is to simply experience a new approach to reading."

Wherever I teach PhotoReading, I find the same attitudes in successful PhotoReaders. People who "try hard to do really well" with

PhotoReading often strap themselves with a big responsibility. Right away, they feel a personal obligation to prove or disprove the whole mind reading system. That is like wanting to take the final exam in calculus before you have learned how to add—and then claiming that you are lousy in math.

You do not have to believe everything about PhotoReading up front. A little skepticism about the technique is fine. No number of testimonials can replace the results you produce with your own efforts. Be willing to give PhotoReading a fair trial and remain open for pleasant surprises. A requirement for success is an open mind.

I urge people to ease into the experience of PhotoReading—to play, embrace confusion, and tame the gremlins. Ironically, it is when we stop trying so hard to succeed that our intuition flowers and we rekindle our natural skill at learning. When we let go of success or failure, we start to get what we want.

When will I attain the levels of comprehension I need?

Remember that the PhotoReading whole mind system is based on multiple passes through printed material. First, we set a purpose and preview. That can be followed, as we choose, by PhotoReading, postviewing, super reading and dipping, skittering, and rapid reading.

Comprehension comes in layers. Previewing gives us a sense of structure. By using the remaining steps of the system, we build on that foundation, gaining a level of comprehension that is consistent with our purpose. This approach frees us.

Perhaps this feels like full comprehension is delayed—that you are not getting the "goodies" from your reading as soon as you want them. My suggestion is to greet this feeling with the NOPS formula and discover what emerges.

Notice it.
Own it.
Play with it.
Stay with it.

For example, a PhotoReader took a seminar during his doctoral program in which he had to read twenty thousand pages. Most students in that program take between six and nine months to finish the required reading and write the necessary papers. For an entire week he previewed and PhotoRead. The next week he tried to activate the books and write his papers; nothing came to him. He expected to know the material. In frustration, he let it all go, feeling he had wasted the week.

The following week the PhotoReader experimented with entering the "beginner's mind." He once again activated the books, astonished that this time everything made sense to him. His writing flowed, and he finished the course, receiving an A for his work. His total investment was only three weeks from the time he started.

Was the second week of activation a waste? Or was it the essential period of incubation and fine-tuning necessary to achieve the end result?

A PhotoReading student described his experience like this:

"I realized that when using the PhotoReading whole mind system, I am actually adding time to do extra things to my reading. I naturally resisted. I could just start reading and comprehending as I go. Or, I could use this new system—adding time to preview and PhotoRead before I could activate for comprehension. My natural response was, why? Why not just get into it?

"I've been telling my kids for years that you have to invest a little bit extra in the learning curve up front before the payoff comes. When you go to school, it is not the information you need. What you are really learning is how to learn—so when you get into the real world, you will be able to get where you want to go in life. Here, I had been giving this advice without taking it myself!

"I soon discovered that the few minutes I invested up front paid back huge dividends. I could save hours reading reports by taking five minutes to preview and PhotoRead. I could save ten to eighteen hours or more on books that used to take twenty hours to read regularly."

In summary this chapter helped you learn the following:

• The NOPS formula—Notice it, Own it, Play with it, Stay with it—will help overcome frustrating habits that prevent learning.

• The beginner's mind is the perfect mindset to maintain during the PhotoReading whole mind system.

Read Bullets

• There are four levels of the learning process you must progress through when learning a new skill.

• Confusion is an appropriate experience during any learning activity.

• The PhotoReading whole mind system uses flow states of consciousness.

• Dr. Lozanov's accelerative learning is a model for the PhotoReading whole mind system.

- We use all eight intelligences described by Dr. Gardner with the PhotoReading whole mind system to make reading multidimensional and more useful.

- The expanded database we access while PhotoReading outweighs the database of the conscious mind by ten billion to one.

- The goal of comprehension is achieved in layers. Paradoxical as it may seem, to achieve your goal, you must let it go.

The PhotoReading whole mind system works. You must use it to demonstrate the benefits in your own life. After you have enjoyed how easily you can produce results with PhotoReading, you might consider how your inner mind can become an active ally in personal development. In Chapter 13, you will explore powerful next steps by learning directly from the authors.

A male PhotoReader PhotoRead a couple dozen books on women's health issues over several weeks. He did no structured activation. Several months later his sister-in-law had a hysterectomy after a troubled birth. He surprised himself and his family with the depth of knowledge he had on fibroid tumors and endometriosis, the primary cause of the problems.

An executive went from being computer illiterate ("I mean, I barely even type!") to a daily user of his computer by PhotoReading computer books, magazines, and manuals. "After about a month of doing this, I suddenly realized that those stupid machines were starting to make sense!"

A CPA attended a continuing education seminar for her profession. Since she arrived early, she had the luxury of reviewing the handout materials before the presentation. Entering the PhotoFocus state she quietly and quickly reviewed the materials. As the day progressed she realized she had a firm grasp of the subject even though she had not previously studied it. She attributes the immediate comprehension of the material to having PhotoRead the handouts.

A copyeditor repeatedly PhotoRead a Thesaurus. His supervisor commended him for a marked improvement in his speed and clarity of writing.

An executive blasts through his daily email in three minutes, instead of avoiding the task and letting them accumulate.

13

Discover Your Genius
Potential with Direct Learning

At Learning Strategies Corporation, we often ask our clients, "Now that you can PhotoRead, what else can your brain achieve?" When they realize we are serious, they begin asking us, "What is the next step beyond PhotoReading?"

Since first developing the PhotoReading seminar, I have discovered ways to access remarkable abilities that extend PhotoReading far beyond merely gathering information. Three concepts presented here can help you to examine and enjoy powerful new skills right away.

Experience the miracle of "direct learning"

In the early days of teaching PhotoReading, we were surprised when graduates reported spontaneous improvement in skills such as tennis, golf, racquetball, piano playing, typing, and public speaking to name a few. The anecdotes invariably involved syntopic reading. When a PhotoReader syntopically read books relating to topics of intense personal interests, somehow actual skill development occurred.

These reports of spontaneous skill development strongly challenged the conventional wisdom in adult education. I had been taught that knowledge acquisition and skill development are two very different learning activities. But evidence was pushing me to consider that behavioral learning could emerge even though no physical practice of the behaviors took place.

My colleagues and I hypothesized that because PhotoReading routes information into the brain preconsciously, somehow the brain must create neuronal links for behavior as it does for cognition.

Literature on the phenomenon of "implicit learning"—learning without conscious or "explicit" memory—suggested our hypothesis might be right on target.

The distinction between explicit and implicit learning can be thought of as the difference between what your head knows and what your body knows. Explicit memory involves learning with awareness and knowing facts that you can recall through consciously directed remembering. Implicit (or implied) memory involves learning without awareness and knowing how to perform skills without being able to describe how you do it.

According to neurologist Richard Restak, M.D., different parts of the brain are involved in the two types of memory. In fact, it has been demonstrated that a person with brain damage to the explicit learning part of the brain can still learn to perform tasks even though they have no conscious recollection of having learned them.

Could it be that PhotoReading naturally activates the implicit learning and memory system of the brain? To test this idea, a medical doctor from South Africa, Izzy Katzeff, suggested that brain studies be performed to track the parts of the brain activated during PhotoReading. A team of medical doctors at the U.S. Veterans' Administration Hospital took up the challenge.

The research team, headed by nuclear medicine specialists Irma Molina, M.D., and Sandra Gracia, M.D., performed brain studies on PhotoReaders. The results of their study with a small subject sample encouraged the research committee to seek additional studies.

In the meanwhile, consider that after PhotoReading several books on a skill you are interested in developing, the skill can suddenly show up in the situations when you need it. We can think of this implicit learning as a sort of spontaneous activation happening behaviorally. "Direct learning" is our systematic approach to capitalize on the phenomenon of direct behavioral activation.

Follow these steps for direct learning

Here is how you perform the direct learning exercise on your own:

• Know what new behaviors you desire. The more specific you can be, the better this process will work. It should be something you have a strong personal desire to learn.

• Select several books that speak authoritatively about the subject. It is important that these books teach the new behaviors you want in a practical, how-to fashion. Books on theory can be helpful, as long as they discuss practical application. Each book represents several years of the author's knowledge and skills and the essential ideas from many books. Imagine that you are downloading this into your neural circuitry.

• PhotoRead your books. Remember to state your purpose clearly before each book and to say a solid closing affirmation after each one. It may be a good idea to take a brief stretch or drink water between books. Allow yourself to remain centered and relaxed throughout the process. If something happens to distract you between books, take a few moments to get back into state.

• Direct your mind to generate the behaviors. Remember how you imagined doing things as a child? You called it "Playing Pretend." Gestalt therapists call it "Playing As If." Seeing a mental simulation of the future encodes the brain with the necessary information to give rise to the behaviors according to your needs. This is the direct learning activation stage. The information will be activated spontaneously in the appropriate contexts. The complete procedure for direct learning can be found in my *Natural Brilliance* book.

When performing the direct learning process, I suggest not activating your books consciously because the conscious mind tends to interfere by trying to control the process. You see, most people in our culture have been schooled in the "Puritan Work Ethic," which means "You must work hard to achieve rewards." Your athletics coach may have said "No pain, no gain" to reinforce the idea that hard work, effort, and struggle are the fastest routes to success. Direct learning challenges such traditional assumptions by demonstrating that the inner mind can provide a "path of least resistance" to our success. Since living life effortlessly is a real human option, why not go for it?

In summary, the direct learning process invites you to answer the simple question, "What do you want?" When you can answer that question with clarity, you are well on your way to accomplishing your desires. With direct learning, you PhotoRead a stack of books that encourages the use of the skills you need. Then, you imagine yourself in the future, in the moment of enjoying the accomplishment of your goal. This tells your brain to spontaneously generate the behaviors you need to achieve your future success.

Think of your brain as an ally in personal and professional development. Ask it to help, and trust it to demonstrate the wonders it can perform for you.

Use the Natural Brilliance model

You can realize your genius potential with ease. PhotoReading gets you started. The four-step Natural Brilliance model for lifelong learning keeps you on track.

Natural Brilliance is a process for consistently breaking through to success in areas of your life where you may feel stuck. The steps are: Release, Notice, Respond, and Witness. I cover these steps in detail in my book *Natural Brilliance: Moving from Feeling Stuck to Achieving Success* and in the *Natural Brilliance Personal Learning Course*.

The first step, Release, drains stress out of the physical systems. Relaxing your body and mind is the essential first step to promote the optimal state for learning—relaxed alertness.

Tension and resistance characterize a person trying to change the present situation. Paradoxically, tension and stress cause us to narrowly focus our attention. We manage micro-details and miss the big picture.

You can release in many ways. Changing posture, eye-focus, breathing, and thoughts can produce a calming effect. By draining stress out of the body and mind, you automatically minimize the behaviors that keep you stuck. Simultaneously you restore the natural acuity of your sensory systems, giving you access to new information and choices.

Release lets you pull your forehead off the tree long enough to see that you are in the forest. When you put your sensory systems back online, you step out of tunnel vision and the world opens up.

The second step, Notice, means entering a state of increased awareness and paying attention to information in the present situation. When you attend to the input in your sensory systems, you will naturally generate creative options and promising responses.

The speed of the mind is tremendous. The inner mind works at making associations much faster than the conscious mind can duplicate. When given the proper direction, the whole mind can accomplish virtually any problem-solving task.

A person in a stuck state oscillates between wanting to push forward and pull back at the same time. This happens when a goal is desired but potential failures or punishments must be avoided. The combination of releasing and noticing allows you to step out of the oscillation and stuck state.

Noticing involves becoming aware of what is happening around and in you. It helps you develop a new point of view, a perceptual position in which you can see what you are doing in the situation in which you are doing it. Then, from the rich information about your outer experience and inner experience, you can make decisions and respond to people and events.

An "outside yourself" awareness opens the possibility for balance. A stuck state is like running back and forth on a seesaw on the school playground. With the step of Notice, you hop off and choose a new position to work from—alongside the oscillating system. It is much easier to minimize the oscillation and bring the teeter-totter into balance.

By combining the steps of Release and Notice, you achieve the optimal learning state, the state of relaxed alertness. Once you have developed relaxed alertness and increased your foundation of information, you can choose new responses from a rich set of options.

Step 3, Respond, involves taking action to discover how things change. Any response either increases the oscillation and the inability to move, or it dampens the oscillation and increases movement toward a satisfying outcome. Your actions will either make the situation better or it will not. In either case, movement within a system provides real and immediate feedback.

Once your brain recognizes your doing (or not doing) something makes your situation better or worse, you have the beginnings of change and the first step in gaining control of the outcomes you want to produce. When you feel you can cause your life to get better, you can generate a positive effect that builds self-confidence and self-esteem.

Witnessing the results of your actions, Step 4 of the model, puts you in charge of producing the success you want. When you witness, you find a nonjudgmental position from which you observe learning taking place. Whether your response in Step 3 has succeeded or failed is not significant. The important thing is to get feedback that can lead to learning. In this step the feeling is one of safety and blessing.

Do you desire to break through to a new level of performance? The Natural Brilliance model leads you to replicate and reclaim the safety and blessings of your natural learning genius.

Unfortunately, many of us experienced school as a place of wounding. Natural Brilliance will assist you in overcoming your wounds and replacing them with the strengths of safety and blessing. The great opportunity for you as an adult is to witness your continued learning each day. As you develop the Natural Brilliance in you, the results you create will shine throughout your life.

If you ever feel stuck when learning to use part of the PhotoReading whole mind system, use the four steps of Natural Brilliance. Release the push and pull of trying to do it right. Notice more of the rich information around and within you. Respond in new and creative ways that lead to greater ease and flow. Witness the results you produce and stay on track to your goals.

Awaken your intuition

In the first public PhotoReading seminar in January 1986, I asked a question at the beginning of our third session: "What different or unusual experiences have you noticed since beginning to PhotoRead?"

Tom, who had been fairly shy up to that point, stood up boldly and said, "I don't know if this has anything to do with PhotoReading, but I was hoping maybe you could explain this to me. I am a volunteer fireman. On Wednesday night last week, I awoke to the fire alarm, got dressed, and went over to the station. I was surprised to find that I was the first person there. I had never been first before. I stood there a minute, and suddenly the alarm went off. I had actually responded to the alarm ten minutes before it went off! Can you explain how this happened?"

For years, I had taught seminars designed to help people gain access to their intuitive powers. Tom's uncanny experience typified how people's intuition can spontaneously awaken. What appeared as an improbable coincidence was a demonstration of how the finely tuned inner mind can communicate in a purposeful way.

When you PhotoRead and activate, you increase the communication between your conscious and nonconscious mind. That is exactly what intuition is—the conscious communication of nonconscious perceptions. Here is how you can increase access to your own intuitive awareness:

• Explore the sensory representations inside you including your inner pictures, inner dialog, and inner feelings.

• Notice information at the periphery of your awareness by opening your peripheral vision. Listen to multiple auditory information such as several conversations in busy places like restaurants, and the multiple voices on Paraliminal CDs. Also notice subtle kinesthetic experiences. For example, right now notice the feeling of how you are sitting, your emotions, and the temperature on the back of your neck.

- Be curious and receptive to information coming to you from your external and internal environments.

- Play games with your intuition. When standing at a bank of elevators, push the call button, and guess which one will open first.

The dual benefit to you for awakening your intuition includes enhancing your PhotoReading and activation skills while simultaneously enriching the quality and ease of your life.

A 13-year-old boy attended the first PhotoReading course in Mexico. Although he had been sighted in only one eye since birth, he eagerly applied the skills of PhotoReading. A month after the course, one of his teachers asked, "Does PhotoReading really work for you?" His response was to hand her his dictionary, which he had PhotoRead several times. He told her, "Give me any word, and I will tell you where the word is positioned on the page." He correctly identified the position of nine out of ten words, to which the teacher responded, "Hmmm, maybe it does work!"

An electrical engineer at a large power generating utility found himself contributing in a meeting—actually leading the group—on a topic for which he had almost no experience. He was baffled by his obvious expertise. When back in his office, he wondered where his sudden influx of knowledge came from. Then he noticed a stack of trade journals on his shelf that he had recently PhotoRead. Sure enough, the most recent journal contained an in-depth analysis of the meeting's topic.

A postal employee entered zip codes into a computer while at the resource level. He became more relaxed and made fewer mistakes than before.

A home-brewer PhotoRead a new book on beer-making. That night he dreamed of a new recipe, which he later tried. It was his best batch to date.

An average student PhotoRead a novel for a literature exam and scored 100 percent.

A minister PhotoRead a section of the Bible before sleeping one evening. He dreamed about a Bible story and how it related to a problem in the life of one of his parishioners. He was able to use his insights to counsel the parishioner.

14

The Secret of the PhotoReading Whole Mind System

The true secret of PhotoReading at 25,000 words a minute is that you already have the ability. Your brain is hardwired for genius. Rediscover your natural genius. Play with it, and allow it to become part of your everyday life.

Actively encourage yourself. You will discover that you have abilities reaching far beyond PhotoReading.

A call to active reading

I am privileged to have studied the most masterful learners in the world—babies. Babies are active, purposeful, goal-oriented, insatiable learners. My wife and I have loved watching our three children engage the physical and mental universe. Their hunger to make sense of life is enormous.

Although our three boys are now well beyond the baby stage, they still actively explore their world. Learning is active; activity is the fuel of genius. Our genius fades when passivity takes over.

Television teaches us to be passive. It tells us to wait; everything we want will come to us—right after this commercial. If reading becomes passive, our genius is stifled.

Regardless of what type of reading you do, stay active. The more active you are, the more fluent your reading becomes and the more effective you will be at achieving the results you desire. Fluent readers maintain a high degree of focus by reading purposefully and by asking questions of the author as they read. Concentration, the essence of active reading, is not nearly so much a discipline as it is an attitude.

Realize that you are reading by choice and that you want to create value for yourself. Choice makes a real difference in how easily you accomplish your purpose for reading, be it a desire to gain information and skills, to evaluate ideas, or to simply relax. When you consciously choose to read, you engage your mind's full capability.

As I write these words, I think of Georgi Lozanov, the grandfather of accelerative learning. Early in his career, Lozanov believed the purpose of his methods was to eliminate fear from the classroom and increase people's suggestibility—their ability to receive information on a nonconscious level. Over the years, his thinking changed, and his overriding goal became to offer learners more choices.

This is precisely the aim I have for you in reading. My goal in this book has been to lay out a new paradigm for reading and an accompanying set of tools that maximize your choices when interacting with the printed page.

Make the PhotoReading whole mind system your ally as you become a more active, purposeful, and demanding reader. Read with speed and efficiency. Take the opportunity to extend your understanding beyond your current limits. Above all, use your mind's full potential to accomplish your personal and professional goals, and discover an abiding joy in the process. You can do it!

A new scenario, a closing thought

Remember the scenario of choice from Chapter 2? Let us return to it for a moment. You are ready to enjoy any part of it you desire.

You begin each workday feeling on top of the information needed to make effective and timely decisions. Whenever you read, you do so with a sense of effortlessness and relaxation. You find it easier to win approval for your proposals because your recommendations are backed by solid evidence.

Reading technical reports, a task that used to consume hours, now requires only minutes per document. At the end of your day you look at a clear desk feeling ready for the following day.

This quality extends to your home life as well. Gone are the piles of untouched books, magazines, newspapers, and mail that once crowded your living space. You keep up with the latest daily news in 10 to 15 minutes a day. In a single sitting you pare down or eliminate your "to be read" piles. And with the extra time, you consistently complete the top-priority tasks on your to-do lists.

Your advanced reading abilities enable you to take courses, complete degrees, gain promotions, learn new skills, expand your knowledge, and satisfy your general curiosity. The ease of it all makes learning fun. You create time for novels, magazines, and pleasure reading beyond the immediate demands of your job. In the process, you create free time to play as well.

As you embrace the possibilities, savor the experience. What is your commitment now? What step can you take in the next 24 hours to make more of this scenario a reality for you?

Peter Senge, in his book *The Fifth Discipline,* offers a perfect summary:

The learning process of the young child provides a beautiful metaphor for the learning challenge faced by us all: to continually expand our awareness and understanding, to see more and more of the interdependencies between actions and our reality, to see more and more of our connectedness to the world around us.

We will probably never perceive fully the multiple ways we influence our reality. But simply being open to the possibility is enough to free our thinking.

Change is as inevitable in our lives as it is in the world around us. PhotoReading, a catalyst for personal growth, frees our thinking and expands our awareness to cope effectively with change. With the skills of the PhotoReading whole mind system, PhotoReaders adjust to the changes in their schools, workplaces, professions, societies, nations, global community, and planet.

With PhotoReading, you can actively pursue mastery in the face of change—by choice. Choose now to master any part or all of the PhotoReading whole mind system. Every action you take leads to your personal excellence.

Quick Reference Guide:

Steps of the PhotoReading Whole Mind System

One of the maxims of this book is to forget about "practicing" with the PhotoReading whole mind system. Instead, just use it.

To reinforce what you have learned from PhotoReading, choose another book you want to read and apply each of the steps listed below. The sooner you do this, the better. Either do it now, or set a time now to do it in the next three days.

Use this guide whenever you need to as a refresher.

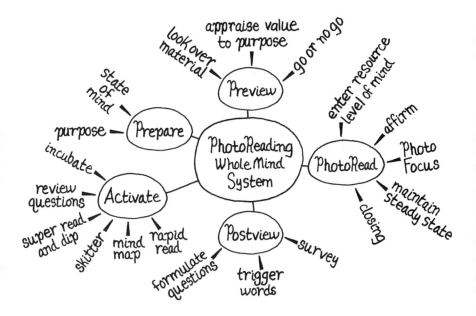

Step 1) Prepare

- Clearly state your purpose for reading.
- Enter the ideal state of mind for learning. This is the state of relaxed alertness.

Step 2) Preview

- Look over the material.
- Appraise the value for your purpose.
- Decide to go or not go further.

Step 3) PhotoRead

- Prepare to PhotoRead.
- Enter the resource level of mind.
- Affirm your personal abilities and the goal you will achieve from these materials.
- Enter the PhotoFocus state by getting a fixed point of awareness (tangerine technique) and the "blip page."
- Maintain a steady state while turning pages and chanting. Keep your breathing deep and even.
- In closing, affirm the impact the information has had and your ability to activate it.

Step 4) Postview

- Now is the time to do a more in-depth survey. You can glance over the table of contents again, perhaps rhythmically peruse the first and last paragraphs of pages or take a look at the index.
- Find trigger words or key terms that attract your attention as you go through the book 10 to 15 pages at a time.
- Formulate questions based on your curiosity and your need to know specific information.

Step 5) Activate

• Ideally, wait a few minutes, or overnight, after PhotoReading before activating. This is a period of incubation.

• Review the questions about the material you wrote down during the postview. This stimulates your mind to begin searching for the connections that lead you to the right sections.

• Super read the parts that attract you. Move your eyes quickly down the center of the page to trigger large blocks of text into conscious awareness. The ideal state of mind for activation is one in which you are attentive to subtle cues in the periphery of your awareness.

• Dip into the text to read selected passages and answer specific questions you asked yourself. The technique of rhythmic perusal is the best way to dip.

• Skitter as an adjunct or alternative to super reading and dipping. After reading the topic sentence of a paragraph, skitter your eyes over the supporting words and phrases that aid your understanding, then read the concluding sentence.

• Create a mind map by making a visual diagram of the key ideas from the written materials.

• Use rapid reading by moving rapidly through the text, reading comfortably from start to finish. Take as much time as you desire. Vary your reading speed depending on the complexity and importance of the material.

• Explore other forms of activation that use multiple intelligences including discussions and dreaming.

Syntopic Reading

1) Establish a purpose.

The first active step of whole mind syntopic reading is to state a purpose that has meaning and value for you.

2) Create a bibliography.

The second active step is to create a bibliography—a list of books that you plan to read. Preview your books to determine if they fit your purpose.

3) PhotoRead all materials 24 hours before activating them.

The mind needs incubation time to create new connections.

4) Create a giant mind map.

Keep your books, a large sheet of paper, and some colored markers on hand for mind mapping. Use mind mapping to take notes during the remaining steps of syntopic reading.

5) Find relevant passages.

Super read and dip through each of the books to find passages that are relevant to your purpose.

6) Summarize these in your own words.

Step back and look at all the passages you have written on your mind map. Briefly summarize what you think the subject is all about using your own terminology.

7) Discover themes.

Look for similarities and differences among the various authors' points of view. What are the predominant themes addressed by all the authors? Make note of these.

8) Define the issues.

Opposing viewpoints between authors are the key issues about your subject. Understanding these points of contention greatly enhances your knowledge on the subject. Super read and dip to find key points related to these issues.

9) Formulate your own view.

In discovering issues, you begin to synthesize your own viewpoint. The skilled syntopic reader looks at all sides and takes no sides at first. After gathering enough information, formulate your own position.

10) Apply.

According to your own needs, apply the knowledge you have acquired.

PhotoReading®

Bibliography

Many books used as reference in the development of the PhotoReading whole mind system were published in the first, second, and third editions of this book. This bibliography contains updated versions of many of those ideas. To obtain a copy of the originally published bibliography, contact the publisher.

Adler, Mortimer J., and Charles Van Doren. *How to Read A Book.* New York: Simon and Schuster, 1972.

Amen, Daniel G. *Change Your Brain, Change Your Life: The Breakthrough Program for Conquering Anxiety, Depression, Obsessiveness, Anger, and Impulsiveness.* NY: Random House, Inc., 1998.

Andrews, Tim. *Where's Your Spotlight? How to enhance learning for others.* Buckinghamshire, England: Stretch Learning, 2004.

Bennett, J. Michael. *Four Powers of Greatness Personal Learning Course.* Minnetonka, MN: Learning Strategies Corporation, 1998.

Barker, Joel. *Future Edge: Discovering the New Paradigms of Success.* New York: William Morrow & Company, Inc., 1992.

Belf, Teri-E, and Charlotte Ward. *Simply Live It UP: Brief Solutions.* Bethesda, MD: Purposeful Press, 1995.

Buzan, Tony. *The Mind Map Book.* New York: Penguin Books, 1996.

Canfield, Jack. *The Success Principles: How To Get From Where You Are to Where You Want To Be.* NY: HarperCollins Publishers, 2005.

Carson, Richard. *Taming Your Gremlin.* New York: Harper Perennial, 1983.

Claxton, Guy. *Hare Brain Tortoise Mind: How Intelligence Increases When You Think Less.* NY: Harper Collins, 1997.

Csikszentmihalyi, Mihaly. *Flow: The Psychology of Optimal Experience.* New York: Harper & Row Publishers, 1990.

Csikszentmihalyi, Mihaly. *Finding Flow: The Psychology of Engagement with Everyday Life.* New York: Harper & Row Publishers, 1997.

Cudney, Milton, and Robert Hardy. *Self-Defeating Behaviors: Free Yourself from the Habits, Compulsions, Feelings, and Attitudes That Hold You Back.* New York: Harper Collins Publishers, 1991.

Davis, Ron D. *The Gift of Dyslexia: Why Some of the Smartest People Can't Read and How They Can Learn.* San Juan Capistrano, CA: Ability Workshop Press, 1994.

Dennison, Gail E., Paul E. Dennison, and Jerry V. Teplitz. *Brain Gym for Business: Instant Brain Boosters for On-the-Job Success.* Ventura, CA: Edu-Kinesthetics, 1994.

DePorter, Bobbi. *Quantum Success: 8 Key Catalysts To Shift Your Energy Into Dynamic Focus.* Oceanside, CA: Learning Forum Publications, 2006.

DePorter, Bobbi. *Quantum Business: Achieving Success Through Quantum Learning.* New York: Dell Publishing, 1997.

Dilts, Robert B. *Strategies of Genius: Albert Einstein.* Capitola, CA: Meta, 1994.

Dixon, Norman F. *Preconscious Processing.* Chichester, NY: Wiley, 1981.

Dixon, Norman F. *Subliminal Perception: The Nature of a Controversy.* New York: McGraw-Hill, 1971.

Dryden, Gordon, and Jeannette Vos. *The Learning Revolution: A Life-Long Learning Program for the World's Finest Computer: Your Amazing Brain!* Rolling Hills Estates, CA: Jalmar Press, 1994.

Edelman, Gerald M. *Bright Air, Brilliant Fire: On the Matter of the Mind.* New York: Basic Books, 1992.

Edelman, Gerald M. *Remembered Present.* New York: Basic Books, 1989.

Edwards, Betty. *Drawing on the Right Side of the Brain.* Los Angeles: J. P. Tarcher, 1979.

Gardner, Howard. *Multiple Intelligences: The Theory in Practice.* New York: Harper Collins Publishers, Inc.,1993.

Gelb, Michael. *How to Think like Leonardo da Vinci.* New York: Delacourte Press, 1998.

Goleman, Daniel. *Emotional Intelligence: Why It Can Matter More Than IQ.* New York: Bantam, 1995.

Gordon, F. Noah. *Magical Classroom: Creating Effective, Brain-Friendly Environments for Learning.* Tucson, AZ: Zephyr Press, 1995.

Harman, Willis, and Howard Rheingold. *Higher Creativity; Liberating the Unconscious for Breakthrough Insights.* Los Angeles, CA: Jeremy P. Tarcher, Inc., 1984.

Hunt, D. Trinidad. *Learning To Learn: Maximizing Your Performance Potential.* Kaneohe, HI: Elan Enterprises, 1991.

Jensen, Eric. *Introduction to Brain-Compatible Learning.* San Diego: The Brain Store, Inc., 1998.

Kandel, Eric R., James H. Schwartz, and Thomas M. Jessell. *Essentials of Neural Science and Behavior.* Norwalk, CN: Appleton & Lange, 1995.

Kline, Peter, and Laurence Martel. *School Success: The Inside Story.* Arlington, VA: Great Ocean Publishers, Inc., 1992.

Kosslyn, Stephen M., and Olivier Koenig. *Wet Mind: The New Cognitive Neuroscience.* NY: The Free Press, 1995.

LaBerge, Stephen, and H. Rheingold. *Exploring the World of Lucid Dreaming.* New York: Ballantine Books, 1991.

LeDoux, Joseph. *The Emotional Brain: The Mysterious Underpinnings of Emotional Life.* New York: Simon & Schuster, 1996.

Levinson, Steve, and Pete C. Greider. *Following Through: A Revolutionary New Model for Finishing Whatever You Start.* NY: Kensington Publishing Corp., 1998.

Margulies, Nancy. *Mapping Inner Space: Learning and Teaching Mind Mapping.* Tucson, AZ: Zepher Press, 1991.

Markova, Dawna. *Open Mind: Exploring the 6 Patterns of Natural Intelligence.* Berkeley, CA: Conari Press, 1996.

Masters, Robert. *Neurospeak: Transforms Your Body While You Read.* Wheaton, IL: Quest, 1994.

McPhee, Doug. *Limitless Learning: Making Powerful Learning an Everyday Event.* Tucson, AZ: Zephyr Press, 1996.

Mindell, Phyllis. *Power Reading: A Dynamic System for Mastering All Your Business Reading.* Englewood Cliffs, NJ: Prentice-Hall, Inc., 1993.

Murphy, Michael. *The Future of the Body: Explorations Into the Further Evolution of Human Nature.* NY: Tarcher/Putnam, 1992.

Norretranders, Tor. *The User Illusion: Cutting Consciousness Down To Size.* NY: Penguin Books, 1998.

Ornstein, Robert. *The Right Mind: Making Sense of the Hemispheres.* NY: Harcourt Brace & Company, 1997.

Ostrander, Sheila, and Lynn Schroeder, with Nancy Ostrander. *Super-Learning 2000.* New York: Delacorte Publishing, 1994.

Perkins, David. *Outsmarting IQ: The Emerging Science of Learnable Intelligence.* New York: Free Press, Simon & Schuster, 1995.

Pert, Candace B. *Molecules of Emotion: Why You Feel the Way You Feel.* New York: Scribner, 1997.

Pinker, Steven. *How the Mind Works.* Pinker, Steven. New York: Norton, 1997.

Promislow, Sharon. *Making The Brain Body Connection: A playful guide to releasing mental, physical, and emotional blocks to success.* West Vancouver, BC, Canada: Kinetic Publishing Corporation, 1999.

Promislow, Sharon. *Putting Out The Fire Of Fear: Extinguish the burning issues in your life.* West Vancouver, BC, Canada: Enhanced Learning & Integration Inc., 2002.

Ramachandran, F.S., and Sandra Blakeslee. *Phantoms In The Brain: Probing the Mysteries of the Human Mind.* New York: Morrow, 1998.

Restak, Richard M. *The Modular Brain: How New Discoveries in Neuroscience Are Answering Age-Old Questions About Memory, Free Will, Consciousness, and Personal Identity.* New York: Macmillan, 1994.

Robinson, Adam. *What Smart Students Know: Maximum Grades. Optimum Learning. Minimum Time.* New York: Crown, 1993.

Rose, Colin, and Malcolm Nicholl. *Accelerated Learning for the 21st Century: The Six-Step Plan to Unlock Your Master-Mind.* NY: Delacorte Press, 1997.

Scheele, Paul. *The PhotoReading Whole Mind System.* Minnetonka, MN: Learning Strategies Corporation, 1997 (2nd ed.).

Scheele, Paul. *PhotoReading Personal Learning Course.* Minnetonka, MN: Learning Strategies Corporation, 1995.

Scheele, Paul. *Natural Brilliance: Move from Feeling Stuck to Achieving Success.* Minnetonka, MN: Learning Strategies Corporation, 1997.

Scheele, Paul. *Natural Brilliance Personal Learning Course.* Minnetonka, MN: Learning Strategies Corporation, 1997.

Secretan, Lance. *One: The Art and Practice of Conscious Leadership.* Caledon, Ontario, Canada: The Secretan Center, Inc., 2006.

Seigel, Robert Simon. Six Seconds to True Calm. Santa Monica, CA: Little Sun Books, 1995.

Shlain, Leonard. The Alphabet Versus the Goddess: The Conflict Between Word and Image. New York: Viking, Penguin Group, 1998.

Smith, Frank. *Reading Without Nonsense. 2nd ed.* Columbia University, New York: Teachers College Press, 1985.

Smith, Frank. *To Think.* Columbia University, New York: Teachers College Press, 1990.

Sprenger, Marilee. *Learning and Memory: The Brain in Action.* Alexandria, VA: Association for Supervision and Curriculum Development, 1999.

Squire, Larry R., and Kandel, Eric R. *Memory: From Mind to Molecules.* NY: Henry Holt and Company, 2000.

Stauffer, Russell. *Teaching Reading as a Thinking Process.* New York: Harper & Row, 1969.

Suzuki, Shunryu. *Zen Mind, Beginner's Mind.* New York: John Weatherhill, Inc., 1970.

Talbot, Michael. *The Holographic Universe.* New York: Harper Collins Publishers, 1991.

Vaill, Peter. *Learning As A Way Of Being: Strategies for Survival in a World of Permanent White Water.* CA: Jossey-Bass Publishers, 1996.

Watzlawick, Paul. *Ultra-Solutions: Or How to Fail Most Successfully.* New York: W.W. Norton & Company, 1988.

Wenger, Win. *Discovering the Obvious.* Gaithersburg, MD: Project Renaissance, 1998.

Wenger, Win, and Richard Poe. *The Einstein Factor: A Proven New Method for Increasing Your Intelligence.* Rocklin, CA: Prima, 1996.

Wilber, Ken. *Integral Psychology: Consciousness, Spirit, Psychology, Therapy.* Boston, MA: Shambhala Publications, 2000.

Wise, Anna. *The High-Performance Mind.* New York: Tarcher, Putnam, 1997.

Wolinsky, Stephen. *Trances People Live: Healing Approaches in Quantum Psychology.* Falls Village, CT: The Bramble Company, 1991.

Wurman, Richard Saul. *Information Anxiety.* New York: Doubleday, 1989.

Wycoff, Joyce. *Mind Mapping.* New York: Berkley Books, 1991.

Index

A

accelerative learning 120, 135
activation 15, 19, 20, 45, 52, 122
  by discussion 87, 88
  dip 55. *See also* dip
  dreams 100. *See also* dreams
  electronic files 77
  email 77
  journals 76
  magazines 76
  manual 72
  mind mapping 62. *See also*
    mind mapping
  newspapers 76
  novels 76
  rhythmic perusal 58
  skittering 61, 72
  spontaneous 69, 72
  super read and dip 55
  textbooks 77
  with group discussion 87
active reading 134
Adler, Mortimer 104
affirmations 37, 45
"aha!" experience 69. *See also*
  spontaneous activation
ask questions 49
associations 53, 64, 72
attention 23, 48
  seven units of 26
attitudes 16, 115, 123

B

Bacon, Francis 24
barriers 13, 82
beginner's mind 114, 125
benefits 8
Bennett, J. Michael 58, 61
blip page 41. *See also* PhotoFocus
brain channels 95
brain frequency 95
Buzan, Tony 63. *See also* mind
  mapping

C

Carson, Richard 112
chanting 43
choice
  importance to reading 14, 135
comprehension 2, 3, 5, 14, 23, 25,
    52, 55, 57, 61, 64, 65, 67, 68,
    72, 78, 115, 123
  how to achieve 124
  levels of conscious
    comprehension 52
concentration 23, 25, 37, 80, 92, 134
concert session 121
confusion 112, 117, 124
conscious
  competence 116
  incompetence 116
  mind 54, 115, 121
conventional reading 67
Copland, Aaron 123
Csikszentmihalyi, Mihaly 120
curiosity 54

T

taking tests 81
tangerine technique 28
tests 98, 113
time management 25
    prioritize 75
    strategies 75
time required to learn 115
traditional education
    reading 118
train of thought 59
transformations 7
trigger words 19, 54. *See also*
    preview
tunnel vision 40, 130

U

unconscious incompetence 116. *See
    also* stages of learning

V

vision training 93
visual cues 55
visual field 55. *See also* peripheral
    vision
visual memory 64, 93

W

web pages 77
well-formed goals 98. *See also*
    goals
Wenger, Win 122
whole mind 68. *See also* mind
Wycoff, Joyce 63. *See also* mind
    mapping

Z

Zen 94, 96, 115. *See also* meditation

Tools for Lifelong Learning

We publish tools to help you experience your potential. Call for more information on the following programs or visit our website at www.LearningStrategies.com.

PhotoReading Personal Learning Course

The self-study course is not just a recorded seminar, but a comprehensive program designed for personal study. You receive 16 easy-to-follow sessions, the *Memory Supercharger* Paraliminal session, a 68-page course manual, the PhotoReading book, *Natural Brilliance* by Paul Scheele, another book to PhotoRead, and a tuition certificate good toward the PhotoReading seminar. Plus, you can call PhotoReading coaches when you need help at no charge.

PhotoReading Results Supercharger

Soar to higher levels of reading and learning performance with the 3-DVD *PhotoReading Results Supercharger* Pack. You will see three one-hour television documentaries that follow PhotoReading students who take their accomplishments to the next level. Watch six students do the PhotoReading challenge on TV. They will each be given thirty minutes to get through a thick book and be grilled on stage in front of a live audience. See what they do and learn to develop the same confidence and competence.

PhotoReading Seminar

Learn PhotoReading through seminars offered worldwide by certified instructors licensed by Learning Strategies Corporation. Each participant receives a special set of course materials designed specifically for the seminar format. Visit our website for a schedule.

PhotoReading Retreat

Spend five days with Paul Scheele and some of our best instructors in a total immersion to explore the limits of PhotoReading. You will take your skills to the next level of performance and learn how to use PhotoReading to excel in all areas of your life. Notification of the Retreat is made by email.

PhotoReading Instructor Training Course

An intensive training course is offered for people who want to teach PhotoReading. Prospective enrollees must be graduates of the PhotoReading seminar. They must have experience teaching adults and applying the principles of neuro-linguistic programming or related technologies.

EasyLearn Languages

In as little as ten minutes a day you can learn a new language without rote memorization or tedious study. Learn in the same effortless manner you learned your native language. Accelerated learning principles ensure that the EasyLearn method is easier and more fun than any other language program.

Genius Code

Tune into the secret messages your brain automatically sends to dramatically and easily change your life. You can improve your performance in virtually all aspects of mental ability including memory, quickness, IQ, and learning capacity.

Mind development pioneer, Win Wenger, Ph.D., has research showing that the exceptional achievements of famous thinkers may have been more the result of mental conditioning than genetic superiority. He believes he can guide you to condition your own mind in the same way. This means that genius thinking is within your grasp.

Paul Scheele and Win Wenger teamed up to create a fascinating, one-of-a-kind exploration into the human mind with useful and practical applications that can benefit you and your PhotoReading immediately and for a lifetime.

Memory Optimizer

Paul Scheele worked with memory and learning expert Vera F. Birkenbihl to create an innovative self-study to significantly improve your memory. Their unique approach uses "The Birkenbihl Method" and "Paraliminal Learning." Concepts and practical processes such as Intelligent Gap Management, the Inner Archive, Memory Pyramid, and the Anchorman List coupled with 57 memory tricks give strength to your memory and ability to learn. The appendix includes an article on using the *Memory Optimizer* course to improve your PhotoReading activation.

Personal Celebration

Paul Scheele created relaxing and empowering audio programs to help you gain purpose and satisfaction in life. You will meet dozens of friendly people who give you pleasant, life-affirming messages.

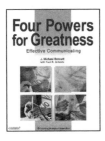

Four Powers for Greatness

Discover the four "power" skills that can stop you cold or lead you to greatness: Listening, Reading, Speaking, and Writing.

When you complete *Four Powers for Greatness* you will be able to quickly and efficiently absorb thoughts, ideas, and feelings by becoming a more effective listener and reader. Plus, you will enjoy the ability to express yourself with powerful speaking and writing skills.

Professor J. Michael Bennett's course includes six recordings and a course manual.

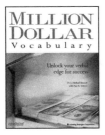

Million Dollar Vocabulary

From the first listening session your vocabulary will grow. Professor J. Michael Bennett and Paul Scheele's *Million Dollar Vocabulary* contains breakthrough processes to make it easier to learn 600 words and their meanings—and use them in every day life. The course consists of 12 lessons on six CDs. The 64-page playbook includes a review of the lessons, quizzes and crossword puzzles, tips for expanding your vocabulary, and an extensive glossary.

The highlights of the course are two Paraliminal learning sessions that will imprint the words and their meanings directly to your brain. Verbally strong people are credited with superior intelligence, higher education, and gifted capabilities.

Genius Mind DVD

Forget boring talks about "brain power"... this is a rock concert of mental potential. You'll see how the brain works and learn how to use this knowledge to further your financial, relationship, and academic success.

Natural Brilliance Book

Everyone feels stuck in some part of life, and this blocks success. Blast away those blocks, and success flows freely.

Using a groundbreaking four-step process, Paul Scheele shows you how to effectively move past feeling stuck and release your natural billiance. You will also learn:

• How to get ahead—and keep going.

• Ways to ensure you achieve your goals.

• New strategies for creativity and problem solving.

• How to create a compelling future of more time and joy.

Natural Brilliance Personal Learning Course

Paul Scheele created a uniquely powerful self-study course to help you overcome blocks. As a result,

• Life becomes smoother and more fulfilling.

• Proverbial mountains shrink to molehills.

• Relationships become more meaningful and pleasurable.

• Stress drains from your life.

• Goals soar to achievement.

See how Natural Brilliance can work for you while listening to the first recording. You will actually work on an area of life in which you feel stuck. On the next four recordings, you will explore the four steps of Natural Brilliance. On Session B of those recordings, Paul guides you through a Paraliminal learning session to make the steps of Natural Brilliance automatic. The sixth, titled the *Natural Brilliance Generator,* helps you spontaneously move through limitations as they arise in the future.

Paraliminal Learning Sessions

Paul Scheele's Paraliminal sessions activate your "whole mind" to create the most receptive brain state for personal transformation. Through a unique blend of music, nature sounds, and multilevel communications, the Paraliminal technology stimulates your genius mind to begin learning how to quickly improve your life and maximize your potential. There are 26 CDs to help you improve performance in any are of your life:

• *10-Minute Supercharger*—Energize your body and mind in minutes to accomplish whatever you choose.

• *Anxiety-Free*—Gain freedom from fears, project strength, and discover the courage to live and create your life with confidence.

• *Automatic Pilot*—Eliminate negative self-talk and vaporize self-sabotage so you automatically function at peak efficiency.

• *Belief*—Eliminate self-defeating habits of mind and install positive, self-empowering beliefs to bring forth the best in all that you do.

• *Break the Habit*—Replace unwanted habits and addictive behaviors with life-enhancing ones to live healthfully and well with more feelings of peace, self-worth, and confidence.

• *Creating Sparks*—Automatically increase the quality of your thoughts and emotions to ignite fun, attraction, and romance in your relationships.

• *Deep Relaxation*—Calm the mind, diminish stress, and eliminate fatigue, enjoying profound and rejuvenating relaxation while revitalizing your body.

• *Dream Play*—Enhance contact with your inner mind and dream world to access inner strength, inspiration, and creative genius.

• *Get Around To It*—Eliminate procrastination and focus on what needs to be done, creating a burning desire from within.

• *Holiday Cheer*—Capture the feelings of a holiday spirit and transform any day into a celebration of life.

• *Ideal Weight*—Establish an excellent relationship with your body and consistently make choices that serve you in attaining and maintaining your ideal weight naturally.

• *Instantaneous Personal Magnetism*—Turn on poise, charm, and sex appeal to make a positive initial impression on those you meet.

• *Memory Supercharger*—Build confidence in the inner workings of your mind to stimulate your memory, develop your concentration, and feel mentally sharp and free from stress.

• *New Behavior Generator*—Break through counter-productive behaviors and instill behaviors of the super-successful so you achieve more by bringing out your full inner resources.

• *New History Generator*—Release negative events from the past, envision the future you desire, and translate good thoughts into actions and tangible results.

• *New Option Generator*—Respond creatively to challenges that stopped you in the past and take consistent actions fearlessly to generate a lasting future of success.

• *Peak Performance*—Incite deep motivation from within to unlock superior levels of performance in any area of your life for long-lasting results.

• *Perfect Health*—Direct your mind as a powerful ally to initiate your body's perfect healing abilities, replenish your energy, and revitalize your life.

• *Personal Genius*—Activate your inner intelligence to accelerate learning and secure the achievement of your goals.

• *Positive Relationships*—Attract, nurture, and maintain satisfying and supportive relationships in all areas of your life.

• *Prosperity*—Open the flow of abundance in your life to create the success you desire.

• *Sales Leap*—Present a positive first impression to others and perform with the winning attitude and skills of the top performers.

• *Self-Esteem Supercharger*—Remove negative influences of other people, situations, and your own self-talk to gain profound confidence.

• *Smoke-Free*—Effortlessly cut back on the habit of smoking and begin a life of freedom and health.

• *Talking to Win*—Increase your confidence and ease while talking naturally in all settings, and become a masterful presenter.

• *Youthful Vitality*—Exude youthful energy and childlike curiosity in all that you do, activating your passions and rejuvenating your body, mind, and spirit.

Paraliminal Accelerator

The *Paraliminal Accelerator* tells you the exact order to listen to the entire library of Paraliminals for overcoming any issue or achieving any goal.

While the Paraliminals increase your personal power by activating your "whole mind," the *Paraliminal Accelerator* gives you a clear map to direct this power toward a goal or issue that is important to you. No more trying to figure it out by yourself. And, after one complete time through the *Paraliminal Accelerator,* you will know the best ways to use the Paraliminals in the future for your ongoing success.

Clear Mind ~ Bright Future

Bring your hopes and dreams into reality with this eLearning program that you can do on your computer. Life is too short to wait a minute longer! In just a couple of hours, international learning expert Paul Scheele will help you discover your guiding purpose in life, sort out what you really want, create a workable path, and get you on your way to manifesting your hopes and dreams.

Abundance for Life

Most of us live in a trance, the illusion of limitation. Paul Scheele will take you on a journey from your familiar world to follow your hopes and dreams. You will free up energy as you awaken anew into a world of abundance, power, and possibility.

This markedly innovative course has 24 CDs including four Paraliminal sessions and seven meditations. You also receive a breakthrough DVD with hours of supportive material and a thorough course manual. While you can finish the course in a couple of weeks, you could study its principles for a lifetime.

Resiliency

The power to bounce back. Use *Resiliency* strategies to overcome adversity and thrive in most circumstances. Get both the edge to handle life's annoyances and setbacks as well as confidence to deal powerfully with cataclysmic events. Al Siebert and Paul Scheele help you build mental and emotional flexibility to turn misfortune into good fortune.

Boundless Renewal

Don't let the speed of life get the best of you. Rescue yourself from feeling overwhelmed, burned out, disengaged, or out of control with Bernie Saunders and Paul Scheele's *Boundless Renewal*. Use these breakthrough insights and strategies to bring greater emotional, intellectual, and spiritual balance to your life.

Your course includes six audio recordings, including a Paraliminal session, a comprehensive 56-page course manual, a journal, and a special package that holds the secrets to boundless renewal. See what happens when you shift your life's focus from the ever ticking clock to something more valuable.

Spring Forest Qigong

For thousands of years, the Chinese elite have known that controlled breathing combined with focused concentration and simple movements can significantly improve one's health. They have called this practice Qigong (pronounced "Chee-Gong").

Qigong Master Chunyi Lin has demystified this ancient practice and made it practical for today's modern people. His *Spring Forest Qigong Personal Learning Course* guides you through learning simple, easy-to-follow exercises for a vibrant sense of energy and well-being. The Level 1 course consists of six audio recordings, a DVD, a music CD, and a comprehensive manual.

Two exercises, "Moving of Yin & Yang" and "Breathing of the Universe," are particularly effective for PhotoReading and general learning.

Spring Forest Qigong, Level 2, teaches you how to help others heal. It includes four audio recordings, 1 DVD, two music CDs, and a comprehensive manual.

Euphoria!

Seven experts come together to help you experience a natural, euphoric high. Learn to enter, at will, a sense of inner calm. Experience joyful flowing with the events around you. Feel blissful happiness, love, rapture, and peace of mind.

Paul Scheele presents a Paraliminal session, Hale Dwoskin teaches the Sedona Method, D. Trinidad Hunt helps you find your purpose, Chunyi Lin presents a Spring Forest Qigong meditation, Bill Harris gives you a Holosync experience, and Rex Steven and Carolyn Sikes take you on a ride with the Attitude Activator—giving you the gift of a healthful, balanced, and energetic life.

Effortless Abundance: The Alchemy of Wealth DVD

The secret to wealth is knowing where your true power resides. Most people try to build wealth through conscious efforts. Paul R. Scheele, master of the mental makeover, says, "stop it" and shows you how to step out of the limited conscious mind's feeble attempt to control your life. He helps you access a powerful—yet seldom used by everyday people—way of thinking that produces miraculous results. This empowering DVD program, which includes more than a dozen special features that work directly with your genius mind, helps you break free of self-imposed limitations so your infinite intelligence can create the abundant life you choose.

Love and Long Life: The Mars and Venus Connection DVD

Renowned relationship expert and best-selling author John Gray uses his phenomenal metaphor of "men are from Mars and women are from Venus." He explains the difference between men and women and gives concrete advice for creating the brain chemistry of health, happiness, and lasting love. Based on cutting-edge research from his book "The Mars and Venus Diet and Exercise Solution," John shares new findings of gender-specific solutions for optimizing brain chemistry, diet, exercise, stress management, and romance.

Your Healing Power DVD

This DVD follows a 6-day retreat led by teacher and healer Chunyi Lin and organized by Learning Strategies. In *Your Healing Power*, you'll see practitioners use Spring Forest Qigong, hear their commentary and personal insights, and witness miraculous healings. You will learn a soothing chant that helps heal the body, an easy way to reap healthful benefits of fasting, Chunyi Lin's process for helping another person heal, a powerful group healing method that you can use at home, and a sample exercise to experience the healing benefits of Spring Forest Qigong.

Diamond Feng Shui

Discover the enlightening world of Diamond Feng Shui, a revolutionary, yet straightforward, system to attract positive energy and deflect negative energy in your life. For thousands of years, Chinese emperors had access to sacred knowledge about how surroundings affect energy—for better and for worse. They called this knowledge Feng Shui, which means "wind" and "water." In this accessible and powerful course, you'll learn step-by-step how to change the energy of your home or workplace for immediate, long-lasting results in the four main areas of your life: success, relationships, health, and spiritual growth.

Sonic Access

Sonic Access truly is the most mind-blowing personal transformation program we've ever published. In one extraordinary program, we've brought together Paul Scheele's unique Paraliminal technology, the cutting-edge audio frequencies of Holosync, the energy principles of *Diamond Feng Shui*, and the healing sounds of *Spring Forest Qigong*, all wrapped up in the most beautiful and transformative music you will ever experience.

In-House Training

Learning Strategies Corporation offers in-house training that elicits more from the student's brainpower. We use cutting-edge training methods that employ the student's whole mind and body in learning. The programs include PhotoReading, Natural Brilliance, Creative Problem-solving, Accelerated Learning/Faculty Training, Higher Order Thinking, and Memory.

How to Order or Enroll

You may order or enroll through the telephone, fax, mail, email, our secure website, or visiting us in person.

If you do not already have a catalog and order form or enrollment materials, please contact us. Tell us which programs interest you so that we can best serve you.

All purchases come with a 30-day satisfaction guarantee, and you will be able to call specially trained coaches for assistance.

We are pleased to serve you.

 Learning Strategies Corporation

Innovating ways for you to experience your potential

2000 Plymouth Road
Minnetonka, Minnesota 55305-2335 USA

Toll-Free 1-888-800-2688 • 1-952-767-9800
Fax 1-952-475-2373

Mail@LearningStrategies.com
www.LearningStrategies.com

Try a Paraliminal CD for $2!

(regularly $29.95)

See next page for details!